EYEWITNESS ◉ GUIDES

PLANT

Blackberries

Red ginseng root

Gerbera
flower

Moss on
decaying wood

Radish

Peppers

Ornamental
dried corn

Ribwort
plantain
seed heads

Opium poppy
seed heads

Redshank
flowers

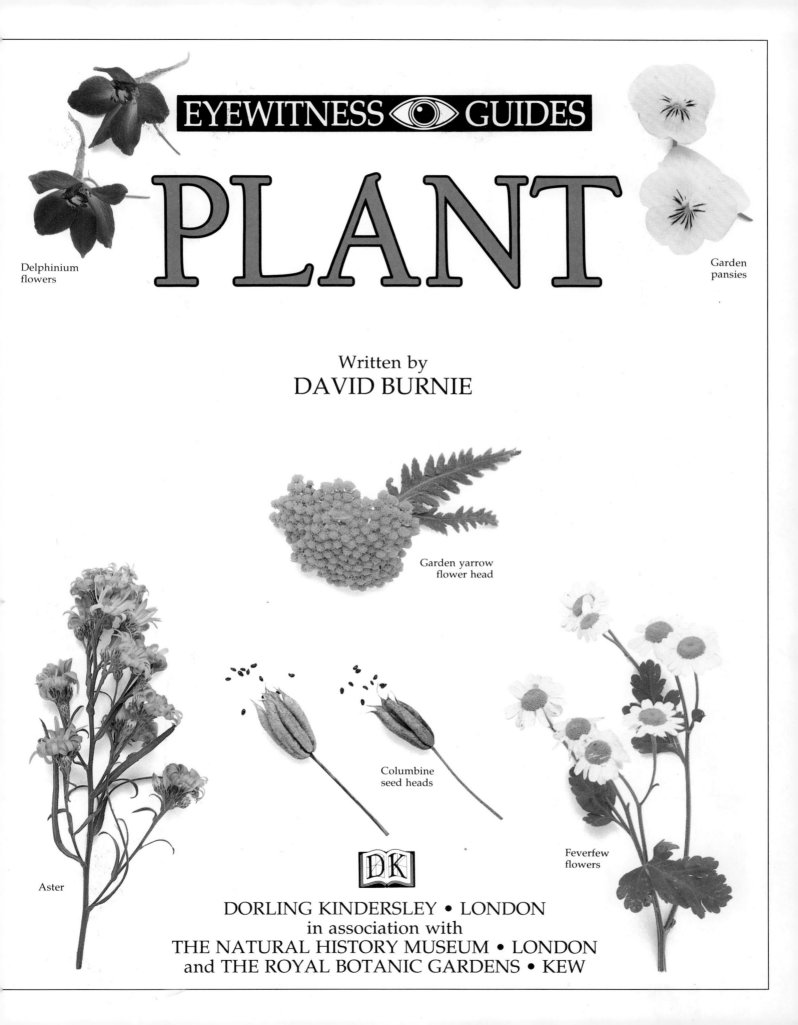

EYEWITNESS GUIDES

PLANT

Delphinium flowers

Garden pansies

Written by
DAVID BURNIE

Garden yarrow flower head

Columbine seed heads

Aster

Feverfew flowers

DK

DORLING KINDERSLEY • LONDON
in association with
THE NATURAL HISTORY MUSEUM • LONDON
and THE ROYAL BOTANIC GARDENS • KEW

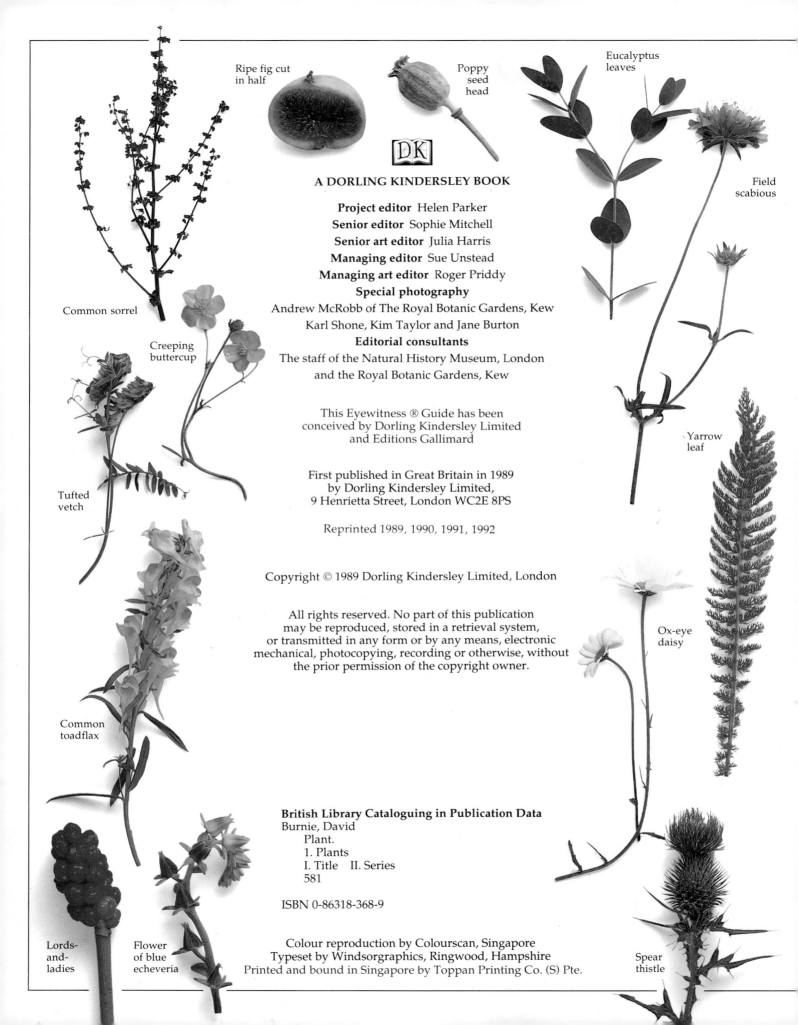

Ripe fig cut in half

Poppy seed head

Eucalyptus leaves

Field scabious

DK

A DORLING KINDERSLEY BOOK

Project editor Helen Parker
Senior editor Sophie Mitchell
Senior art editor Julia Harris
Managing editor Sue Unstead
Managing art editor Roger Priddy
Special photography
Andrew McRobb of The Royal Botanic Gardens, Kew
Karl Shone, Kim Taylor and Jane Burton
Editorial consultants
The staff of the Natural History Museum, London
and the Royal Botanic Gardens, Kew

This Eyewitness ® Guide has been
conceived by Dorling Kindersley Limited
and Editions Gallimard

First published in Great Britain in 1989
by Dorling Kindersley Limited,
9 Henrietta Street, London WC2E 8PS

Reprinted 1989, 1990, 1991, 1992

British Library Cataloguing in Publication Data
Burnie, David
    Plant.
    1. Plants
    I. Title   II. Series
    581

ISBN 0-86318-368-9

Colour reproduction by Colourscan, Singapore
Typeset by Windsorgraphics, Ringwood, Hampshire
Printed and bound in Singapore by Toppan Printing Co. (S) Pte.

Common sorrel

Creeping buttercup

Tufted vetch

Yarrow leaf

Common toadflax

Ox-eye daisy

Lords-and-ladies

Flower of blue echeveria

Spear thistle

Contents

Bladder senna

Young peas in pod

What is a plant?

PLANTS ARE THE KEY to life on Earth. Without them many other living organisms would soon disappear. This is because higher life forms depend on plants, either directly or indirectly, for their food. Most plants, however, are able to make their own food using sunlight. All plants fall into two basic categories. Flowering plants, which this book looks at in some detail, produce true flowers. The non-flowering plants include "primitive" plants, such as mosses, ferns, horsetails, and liverworts, and the "gymnosperms", a group of plants which includes the conifers, like the wellingtonias, shown opposite. There are about a quarter of a million species of flowering plant in the world today, and they grow almost everywhere from snowy mountain slopes to arid desert. This book tells their story.

Lichen

THIS IS NOT A PLANT
It is often difficult to tell simple plants and animals apart. This plant-like organism is a hydrozoan and lives in the sea. Its "branches" are formed by tiny animals called polyps, which have tentacles to trap particles of food.

Lichens growing on limestone rock

THIS IS A PLANT
A lichen is made up of two different organisms: a tiny non-flowering plant called an alga, and a fungus. The algal cells live among the tiny threads formed by the fungus and supply the fungus with food, which they make using sunlight (pp. 14-15). The fungus cannot make its own food and would die without the alga. Lichens grow very slowly and are extremely long-lived.

THIS WAS A PLANT
Forests of horsetails and giant clubmosses, up to 45 m (150 ft) tall, once formed a large part of the Earth's vegetation (right). Over 300 million years, their remains have turned into coal.

Horsetail

CONTEMPORARY COUSINS
Ferns and horsetails are primitive plants and do not have flowers but reproduce by spores. Both first appeared nearly 300 million years ago. Although there are still many types of fern, only 30 species of horsetail live on Earth today.

Spores

Hart's-tongue fern

THE BIGGEST AND THE SMALLEST
The world's most massive plants are conifers - the wellingtonias of California, which can reach heights of over 95 m (310 ft). The smallest flowering plant is the rootless duckweed which is 0.3 mm across.

Ribbon-like "thallus" divides into branches as it grows

Garden pansy

LIVERWORTS
Liverworts are non-flowering plants that live in damp places and reproduce by means of spores.

MOSSES
Mosses do not have flowers. Like liverworts, they reproduce by means of tiny spores.

LIVING SCULPTURES
Algae are simple, non-flowering plants. A diatom is a single-celled alga which has a rigid transparent case, or "frustule", made of silica, a glass-like substance. This microscope photograph shows many species of diatom, each of which has a frustule of a different shape and pattern.

FLOWERING PLANTS
Unlike the other plants on these two pages, these have true flowers. They are also unique in having seeds which develop inside a protective structure called an ovary (p. 17). This later develops into a fruit (pp. 26-27). The garden pansy is a typical flowering plant.

GREEN BLANKETS
Some species of aquatic algae form long chains of cells, creating slimy "blanket-weed".

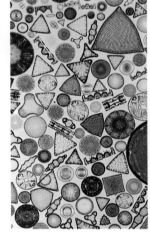

Spirogyra blanket-weed

The parts of a plant

FLOWERING PLANTS ARE BUSY throughout the day and night. During the hours of daylight, the leaves collect the sun's energy. The plant then uses this energy to create food, in the form of sugars (pp. 14-15). This second process is also carried out in the dark. As the food is produced, it has to be transported away from the leaves to the places where it is needed. At the same time, water and minerals, which the roots have absorbed from the soil, have to be carried in the opposite direction to the farthest stems and branches. Respiration, the way in which the plant breathes, occurs throughout the 24 hours, just as in animals. As the plant matures, it embarks on the complicated process of growing flowers, producing and receiving pollen, and eventually setting seed.

Lateral roots

Fine root hairs near the tip of each rootlet absorb water and minerals from the soil

Woody lower stem contains "lignin" which makes it strong

Main root divides to anchor plant in ground

Small shoots that sprout around the base of a larger plant are known as adventitious shoots, or suckers

Lateral root

Main root

New lateral root

Root growth occurs at the tip of each root

Xylem carries water upwards

Phloem carries food to growing tip of root

LOOKING THROUGH A ROOT
In a root, the tube-like cells that conduct water, minerals, or sugars are grouped in the centre. As a root grows, other smaller roots branch off it, helping to absorb water and nutrients, and anchoring the plant in the ground. All roots have a cap of slimy cells at their tip. These cells prevent the roots from being worn away as they grow through the ground.

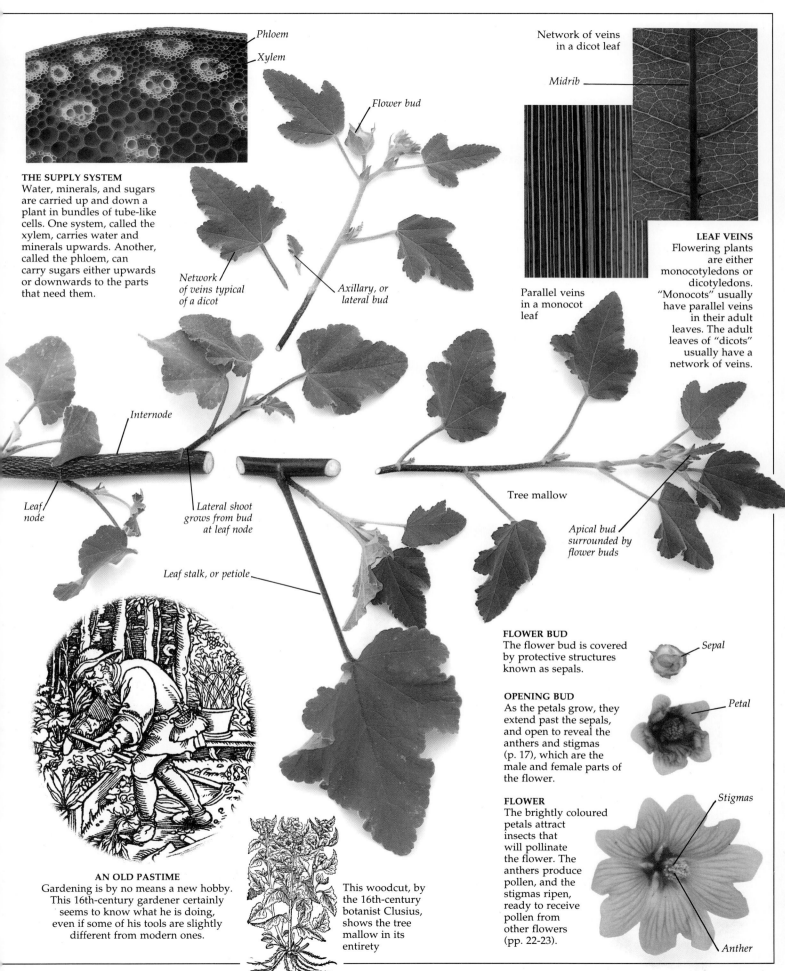

Phloem

Xylem

Flower bud

Network of veins
in a dicot leaf

Midrib

THE SUPPLY SYSTEM
Water, minerals, and sugars
are carried up and down a
plant in bundles of tube-like
cells. One system, called the
xylem, carries water and
minerals upwards. Another,
called the phloem, can
carry sugars either upwards
or downwards to the parts
that need them.

Network
of veins typical
of a dicot

Axillary, or
lateral bud

Parallel veins
in a monocot
leaf

LEAF VEINS
Flowering plants
are either
monocotyledons or
dicotyledons.
"Monocots" usually
have parallel veins
in their adult
leaves. The adult
leaves of "dicots"
usually have a
network of veins.

Internode

Leaf
node

Lateral shoot
grows from bud
at leaf node

Tree mallow

Apical bud
surrounded by
flower buds

Leaf stalk, or petiole

FLOWER BUD
The flower bud is covered
by protective structures
known as sepals.

Sepal

OPENING BUD
As the petals grow, they
extend past the sepals,
and open to reveal the
anthers and stigmas
(p. 17), which are the
male and female parts of
the flower.

Petal

FLOWER
The brightly coloured
petals attract
insects that
will pollinate
the flower. The
anthers produce
pollen, and the
stigmas ripen,
ready to receive
pollen from
other flowers
(pp. 22-23).

Stigmas

Anther

AN OLD PASTIME
Gardening is by no means a new hobby.
This 16th-century gardener certainly
seems to know what he is doing,
even if some of his tools are slightly
different from modern ones.

This woodcut, by
the 16th-century
botanist Clusius,
shows the tree
mallow in its
entirety

A plant is born

A SEED IS A TINY LIFE-SUPPORT PACKAGE. Inside it is an embryo, which consists of the basic parts from which the seedling will develop, together with a supply of food. The food is needed to keep the embryo alive and fuel the process of germination. It is either packed around the embryo, in an endosperm, or stored in special seed leaves, known as cotyledons. For weeks, months, or even years, the seed may remain inactive. But then, when the conditions are right, it suddenly comes alive and begins to grow. During germination the seed absorbs water, the cells of the embryo start to divide, and eventually the seed case, or testa, breaks open. Firstly, the beginnings of the root system, or radicle, sprouts and grows downwards, followed rapidly by the shoot, or plumule, which will produce the stem and leaves.

First true leaves open out

Terminal bud surrounded by next pair of leaves

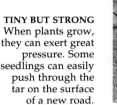

TINY BUT STRONG
When plants grow, they can exert great pressure. Some seedlings can easily push through the tar on the surface of a new road.

First true leaves

Seed coat, or testa, containing seed leaves

Bent plumule

Plumule straightens towards light

3 HARNESSING THE SUN
With the opening of the first true leaves, the seedling starts to produce its own food by photosynthesis (pp. 14-15). Until this time, its growth is fuelled entirely by the food reserves stored in the seed leaves.

First roots grow downwards

1 GETTING GOING
The seed of a runner bean will germinate only if it is dark and damp. First the skin of the seed splits. The beginnings of the root system, the radicle, appears and grows downwards. Shortly after this, a shoot appears, initially bent double with its tip buried in the seed leaves. This shoot, or plumule, will produce the stem and leaves.

2 REACHING FOR THE LIGHT
As the plumule grows longer, it breaks above ground. Once it is above the soil, it straightens up towards the light, and the first true leaves appear. In the runner bean, the seed leaves stay buried. This is known as "hypogeal" germination. In plants that have "epigeal" germination, such as the sunflower, the seed leaves are lifted above ground, where they turn green and start to produce food for the seedling.

Main root grows deeper

Root hairs absorb water and salts from the soil

*First pair of leaves,
now fully grown*

Leaf stalk

GERMINATING GRAIN
Wheat is a monocot, because it
has just one seed leaf (p. 9).
The young shoot grows
upwards through the soil,
protected by a tube called a
coleoptile. As with all
grasses, the growing point, or
"apical meristem", of the
leaves of the wheat plant is
at ground level and can
continue to produce new
shoots at the base of the
plant, even if the leaves are
removed. This is why pasture
can survive being nibbled by
cows, and why lawns thrive
on being mown. Other plants,
such as the bean, have their
growing region, or meristem,
near the tip. If they are
mown or nibbled, they must
grow out from side buds
instead.

Radicle

First leaves emerge

Coleoptile

Roots with root hairs

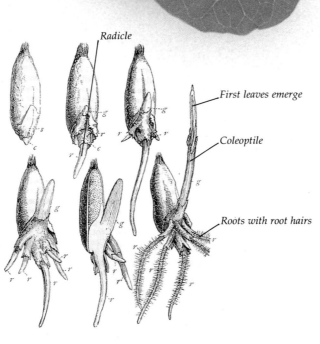

*Fully
upright
stem*

*Seed case is now
redundant and
starts to shrivel*

4 THE RACE TO REPRODUCE
Once germination is complete, the bean grows
quickly. Because it is a climbing plant, it does not need
to develop thick stems. Instead, it uses other plants for
support (p. 38). Given the right conditions, the plant
will produce its first flowers in about six weeks.
After pollination (pp. 22-23) and fertilization,
these will develop into long pods full of seeds.
By the time the seeds have dried out, the life
cycle of the runner bean has turned full circle.

*Thick mass of roots absorbs
water and nutrients from soil*

*Leaves develop from
underground tuber*

A YEARLY CYCLE
Some plants produce
underground storage
organs, such as bulbs,
tubers, and corms
(pp. 32-33). Every
autumn the leaves
of lords-and-
ladies die, but the
following spring
new leaves de-
velop from buds
on the tuber.
Although this
process may look
very similar to
germination, it is
very different.

Bursting into bloom

PLANT LOVERS ARE OFTEN PUZZLED as to why, try as they might, they cannot get their houseplants to flower. A plant may be covered in blooms when it is bought, but the following year it will often produce nothing but a mass of green leaves. The reason for this is that nurserymen treat plants in a particular way to make them flower. All plants have a special control mechanism which makes sure that their flowers develop and open at exactly the right time of year. The main factor that brings a plant into bloom is the length of the night. Some plants will only flower when the nights are long and the days are short (short-day plants). The chrysanthemum, for example, will not flower at all if it is grown indoors in a position where it gets natural light by day and artificial light at night. Other plants, especially those that live far from the equator, only flower at the height of summer, when the days are long. Some flower in any day-length. Once a flower has opened, other mechanisms come into play. Many flowers turn so that they are always facing the sun, and some close up every night, reopening in the morning.

Petals folded back

New petals unfolding outwards

Petal

Sepal

THE FLOWER OPENS
The garden nasturtium belongs to a family of plants that comes from South America. In countries farther from the equator it flowers in mid summer. When the light conditions are right for the plant, flower buds begin to form. Each flower bud is protected by five sepals. As the bud starts to burst, the sepals open to reveal five bright orange petals which grow outwards and fold back. One of the sepals develops a long spur which lies at the back of the flower. This spur produces nectar which attracts insect pollinators to the flower.

BLOOMING LOVELY
Markings called honeyguides show insects the way to the nectar. To reach it, they have to clamber over the anthers (p. 17), which dust them with pollen. As the days pass, the anthers wither and the three stigmas (p. 17) become receptive to the pollen of other plants. Insects in search of nectar now dust the stigmas with pollen.

The life cycles of plants

Flowering plants have very different lifespans, ranging from months to centuries. A common poppy will germinate, flower, set seed, and die, all within a single year. Plants that live in this way are known as annuals. Other plants, such as the wild carrot (p. 55), take two years to complete the same process. They only flower in their second year - the first is spent growing and building up food reserves, which they store in a thick, fleshy root. These plants are known as biennials. Perennial plants are those that live for a number of years. They include species such as the dandelion (pp. 30-31). Perennial weeds are a particular problem for gardeners because their long lifespan gives them time to grow very wide-spreading roots.

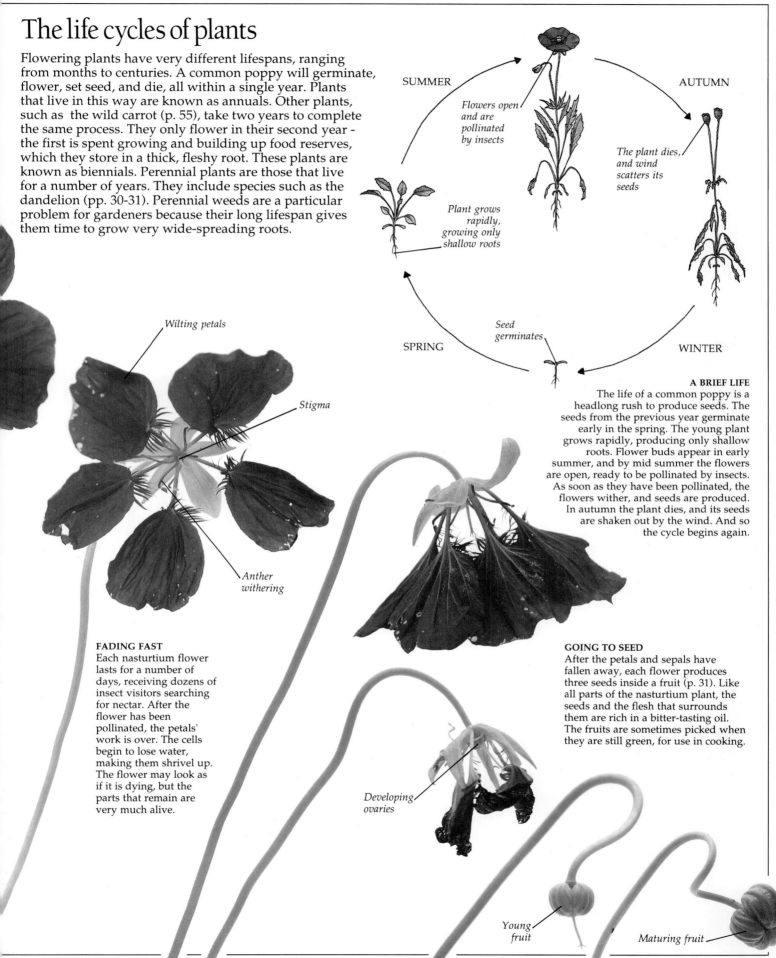

SUMMER

Flowers open and are pollinated by insects

AUTUMN

The plant dies, and wind scatters its seeds

Plant grows rapidly, growing only shallow roots

Seed germinates

SPRING

WINTER

Wilting petals

Stigma

Anther withering

A BRIEF LIFE
The life of a common poppy is a headlong rush to produce seeds. The seeds from the previous year germinate early in the spring. The young plant grows rapidly, producing only shallow roots. Flower buds appear in early summer, and by mid summer the flowers are open, ready to be pollinated by insects. As soon as they have been pollinated, the flowers wither, and seeds are produced. In autumn the plant dies, and its seeds are shaken out by the wind. And so the cycle begins again.

FADING FAST
Each nasturtium flower lasts for a number of days, receiving dozens of insect visitors searching for nectar. After the flower has been pollinated, the petals' work is over. The cells begin to lose water, making them shrivel up. The flower may look as if it is dying, but the parts that remain are very much alive.

Developing ovaries

GOING TO SEED
After the petals and sepals have fallen away, each flower produces three seeds inside a fruit (p. 31). Like all parts of the nasturtium plant, the seeds and the flesh that surrounds them are rich in a bitter-tasting oil. The fruits are sometimes picked when they are still green, for use in cooking.

Young fruit

Maturing fruit

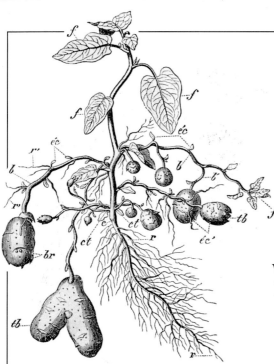

A light diet

UNLIKE ANIMALS, most plants do not need to find food, because they can make it for themselves. The key to the way they do this lies in a green pigment called chlorophyll, which gives them their characteristic green colour. By means of chlorophyll, plants can convert energy from sunlight into chemical energy which can be stored, usually in the form of starch, and used to fuel the growth and development of the plant. The light energy is used to convert carbon dioxide and water into an energy-rich food compound called glucose. This process, known as photosynthesis, works rather like a bonfire in reverse. If you throw a log on to the fire, the carbon that is contained in compounds in the log is reconverted into carbon dioxide gas, and the stored energy is released in the form of heat and light.

UNDERGROUND STORAGE
Potatoes are swollen underground stems, known as tubers, which store the food produced by photosynthesis. This food, in the form of starches, provides the young shoots that develop from buds on the tuber with enough fuel to enable them to grow quickly. Potatoes also provide an important source of human food and they have been bred to produce bigger tubers.

Leaves produced in the dark have little chlorophyll, leaving them pale, or "etiolated"

Potato tuber kept in dark for six months

Stems grow upwards against gravity

A PLANT WITHOUT LIGHT
This potato has spent six months with very little light - conditions which would kill many plants. Because it has been in almost complete darkness, it has not been able to produce any food by photosynthesis. However, it has survived and has even produced some roots and shoots. To do this, the young potato shoots have drawn on the food reserves stored by the parent plant during the previous year's growth. The parent plant used the sun's energy to make food, which it stored in the potato tubers mostly in the form of grains of starch. The young potato plants use the starch to release energy for growth.

Each stem is produced by a small bud, or "eye"

Adventitious roots

Tuber begins to shrink as food stores are used up

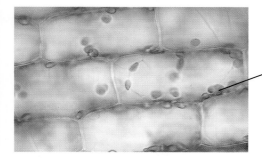

Chloroplasts in cells collect sunlight

A PLANT'S SOLAR PANELS
Inside the cells that make up a plant's leaves are tiny structures called chloroplasts. In a single cell, there may be up to a hundred of them. It is inside the chloroplasts that the green, light-trapping pigment chlorophyll is to be found. The chloroplasts work like minute solar panels, collecting the sun's energy and using it to make food.

Green leaves rich in chlorophyll

STORING SUGAR
Plants store food in various ways - as starches, sugars, or oils. In its first year, an onion plant stores sugars in the onion bulb, which is made up of swollen leaf bases around a shortened stem. In the second year, the sugars in the onion bulb are used up as the plant grows and flowers. Sugars turn brown, or "caramelize", when they are heated strongly, which is why onions darken when they are fried.

RAPID REVIVAL
Three weeks after emerging from the dark, the potato plant is now growing rapidly, and its leaves have turned green. This has happened because more chlorophyll has been made in the leaves to harness the energy of the sunlight falling on them. The growing potato plant is now able to collect enough light to build up its own reserves and it no longer needs the energy stored in the old tuber. If the potato were now planted, the energy gathered by its leaves would be stored in new potato tubers, and the old tuber would shrivel and die.

Stems grow rapidly upwards and turn towards the light

Thickening root system with root hairs

A simple flower dissected

The simplest flowers have the parts arranged in a circle, or whorl

Flowers HAVE BECOME extraordinarily varied during the course of evolution. Nature has produced them in a tremendous wealth of shapes and colours, and to add to this profusion people have bred flowers that are even more brilliant or bizarre than the ones found in the wild. But behind this baffling array of shapes and sizes there is a common pattern. For seed production, all flowers use the same underlying structures. The lily flower shown on these two pages is quite simple - its parts are all separate, and they can all be clearly seen. They fall into three groups. The male parts (the stamens) produce the pollen, the female parts (the carpel) produce the ovules, which will eventually become the seeds. Around both the male and the female parts are sepals and petals which attract insects. When, as in this lily flower, the sepals and petals look the same, they are known as perianth segments, or tepals.

Stamen

Stigma

Petal from inner whorl

Sepal from outer whorl

When sepals and petals look the same, they are known as perianth segments, or tepals

Stamens and stigma packed tightly together

THE LILY FAMILY
The lilies and their relatives make up one of the largest families of flowering plants.

Tepals protecting male and female parts of flower

HOW A FLOWER BUD OPENS
In the lily's flower bud, the male and female parts are packed tightly together inside the protective casing formed by the sepals and petals (tepals). The flower bud opens because certain parts of it start to grow more quickly than others. The inside of the base of each tepal, for example, grows faster than the outside. This forces the tepal to bend outwards at the point where it is connected to the flower stalk. At the same time, unequal growth along the edges of each tepal makes the folds in it open out.

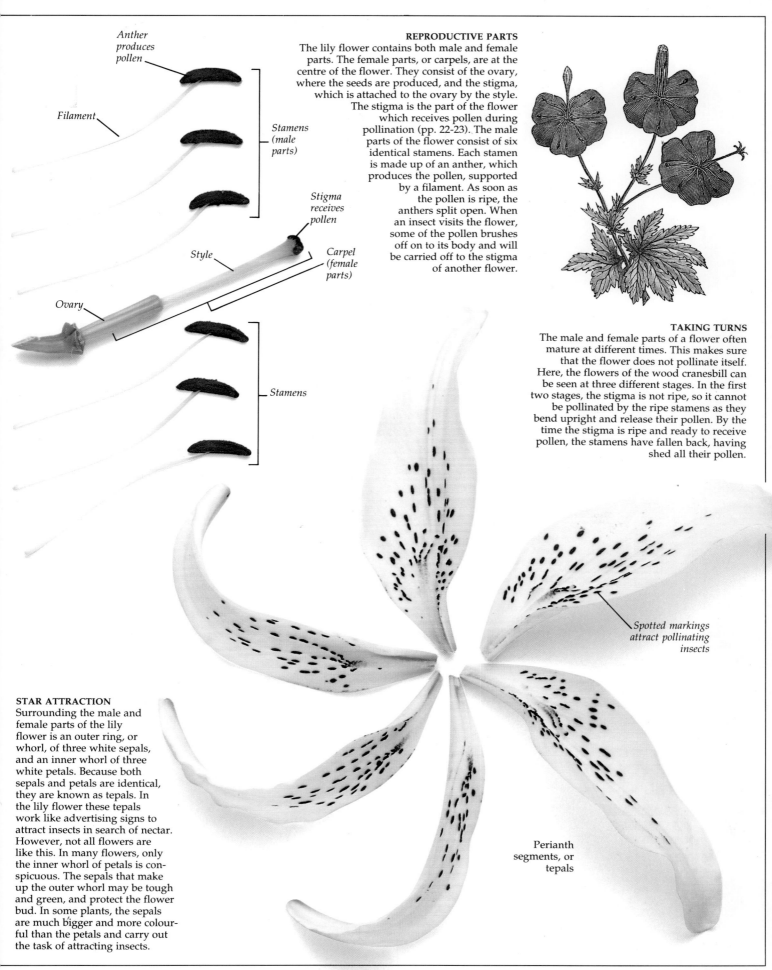

Anther produces pollen

Filament

Stamens (male parts)

Stigma receives pollen

Style

Carpel (female parts)

Ovary

Stamens

REPRODUCTIVE PARTS

The lily flower contains both male and female parts. The female parts, or carpels, are at the centre of the flower. They consist of the ovary, where the seeds are produced, and the stigma, which is attached to the ovary by the style. The stigma is the part of the flower which receives pollen during pollination (pp. 22-23). The male parts of the flower consist of six identical stamens. Each stamen is made up of an anther, which produces the pollen, supported by a filament. As soon as the pollen is ripe, the anthers split open. When an insect visits the flower, some of the pollen brushes off on to its body and will be carried off to the stigma of another flower.

TAKING TURNS

The male and female parts of a flower often mature at different times. This makes sure that the flower does not pollinate itself. Here, the flowers of the wood cranesbill can be seen at three different stages. In the first two stages, the stigma is not ripe, so it cannot be pollinated by the ripe stamens as they bend upright and release their pollen. By the time the stigma is ripe and ready to receive pollen, the stamens have fallen back, having shed all their pollen.

Spotted markings attract pollinating insects

Perianth segments, or tepals

STAR ATTRACTION

Surrounding the male and female parts of the lily flower is an outer ring, or whorl, of three white sepals, and an inner whorl of three white petals. Because both sepals and petals are identical, they are known as tepals. In the lily flower these tepals work like advertising signs to attract insects in search of nectar. However, not all flowers are like this. In many flowers, only the inner whorl of petals is conspicuous. The sepals that make up the outer whorl may be tough and green, and protect the flower bud. In some plants, the sepals are much bigger and more colourful than the petals and carry out the task of attracting insects.

A complex flower

THE FLOWERS on these two pages come from the Himalayan balsam. Although they have the same basic parts as the lily flower shown on pages 16-17, evolution has modified them in different ways so that the two flowers look completely different. Compared with the lily flower, the flowers of the balsam are much more complex and specialized. Himalayan balsam flowers are pollinated by long-tongued insects, such as bees, and they are shaped to ensure that when the insect approaches and enters the flower, it picks up the grains of pollen from the anthers. Bees are attracted to the flower by sugary nectar which is produced in a spur attached to a pouch at the back of the flower. To reach this nectar, a visiting bee first has to land on a platform made up of petals. It then has to climb right inside the flower and stretch out its long tongue. When the bee is in this position, its back touches the anthers. These give it a dusting of pollen which it then carries to the next flower it visits.

Developing flower bud from the side

Developing nectar spur

Flowers develop in clusters and open one at a time

Pouch-shaped third sepal

Nectar spur

Front, or anterior, petal

Sepal

Stigma

Corona of thread-like hairs

Anther

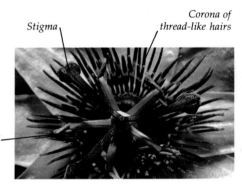

A PAT ON THE BACK
Insects visit passion flowers in search of nectar produced in the base of the flower. When the passion flower opens, the anthers, which are lower than the styles (p. 17), dust pollen on to the insect's back. A few hours later the styles curve downwards so that they are lower than the empty anthers and can collect pollen from another insect's back.

Two petals joined together

ATTRACTIVE TO INSECTS
Himalayan balsam flowers each have three sepals and five petals, and are symmetrical in as far as each half is a mirror image of the other. Two of the sepals are small flaps at the base of the flower. They protect the young flower bud. During millions of years of evolution, the third has become much larger and shaped into a pouch. At the end of this pouch lies the narrow spur which produces nectar.

Fully formed flower from the side

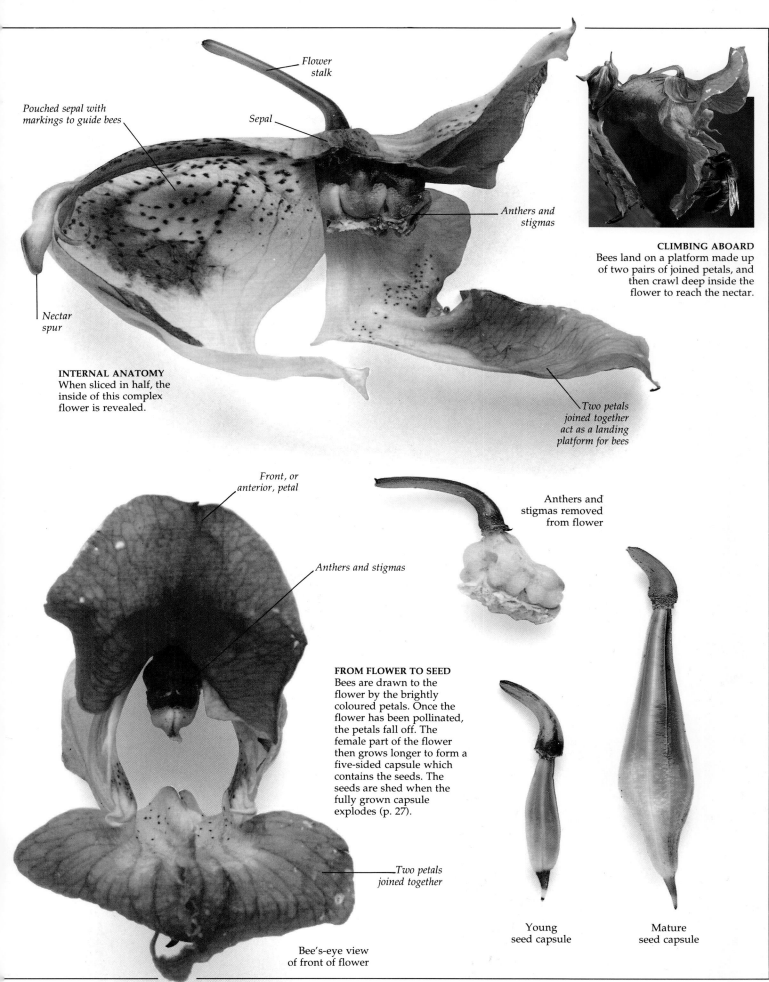

Flower stalk

Pouched sepal with markings to guide bees

Sepal

Anthers and stigmas

Nectar spur

CLIMBING ABOARD
Bees land on a platform made up of two pairs of joined petals, and then crawl deep inside the flower to reach the nectar.

INTERNAL ANATOMY
When sliced in half, the inside of this complex flower is revealed.

Two petals joined together act as a landing platform for bees

Front, or anterior, petal

Anthers and stigmas

Anthers and stigmas removed from flower

FROM FLOWER TO SEED
Bees are drawn to the flower by the brightly coloured petals. Once the flower has been pollinated, the petals fall off. The female part of the flower then grows longer to form a five-sided capsule which contains the seeds. The seeds are shed when the fully grown capsule explodes (p. 27).

Two petals joined together

Bee's-eye view of front of flower

Young seed capsule

Mature seed capsule

All sorts of flowers

Bear's breeches

Petals fused to form a tube

HOW MANY INDIVIDUAL FLOWERS are there on these two pages? The question is not quite as simple as it sounds. You would certainly need a magnifying glass to work out the answer, because the final figure adds up to at least 3,300. Some plants, such as the tulip, each have just a single flower. Others, like the dog rose, have a lot of flowers, but each one develops and blooms separately. Many other plants - including most of the plants on these two pages - produce flowers grouped together in clusters known as flower heads. Flower heads have many different shapes, and they vary widely in size and in the number of flowers they contain. The world's biggest individual flower, produced by the giant rafflesia (pp. 44-45), is completely dwarfed by the world's biggest flower head. This is grown by the rare South American puya, which reaches a height of nearly 10 m (33 ft).

Honeysuckle

Mullein

Rosebay willowherb

Dog rose

Individual flower

Individual flower

REGULAR FLOWERS *above*
A flower is described as being regular if all the flower parts, including the sepals, petals, anthers, and stigma, are positioned on a simple circular plan, like the dog rose above.

The rose on this Tudor coin is based on the dog rose

FLOWER SPIRES *left*
Flowers in spires usually open in sequence, starting at the bottom. This sequence may take a number of weeks to complete. By the time the last flower has opened, the first may already have set seed.

IRREGULAR FLOWERS *right*
An irregular flower is still symmetrical, but in a more limited way. Most irregular flowers are bilaterally symmetrical, meaning that they can be divided into two halves that are mirror images of each other.

The iris is a regular flower which can be cut symmetrically into three pieces

Iris

Sepal

Petal

Sweet pea

Clematis

SHOWY TEPALS
The sepals and petals of some flowers, like the clematis, are so similar that it is difficult to tell them apart. These parts are known as tepals (p. 16) and may be brightly coloured.

Ray floret with single ray

Brightly coloured tepal

NO PETALS?
The ray florets of composite flowers do not always have obvious rays. Most species of chamomile have white rays (right), but in some varieties, although rays are present, they are difficult to see (left).

Disc florets

Eryngo

Eryngo has unusual domed flower heads

COMPOSITE FLOWERS
The flower heads of plants such as sunflowers and daisies are known as composite flowers, because they are composed of many tiny flowers clustered together. Sunflower heads have many hundreds of florets - disc florets in the centre of the flower head, and ray florets, each with a single petal-like "ray", around the outer edge. In the yarrow (below), each flower head is made up of many individual disc florets surrounded by about five ray florets. These flower heads are crowded together to form a bigger cluster with about 1,000 florets in all.

Sunflower

Ray florets

FLOWERS IN UMBELS
Not only are small flowers more visible if they are grouped together, but they also provide a better landing platform for pollinating insects. In plants of the carrot family, such as hogweed (right), flowers are grouped together in umbrella-shaped clusters, called umbels. This family of plants is known as the umbellifers.

Flower head of hogweed

Flower head of cultivated yarrow

How a plant is pollinated

THE FASCINATING SHAPES and brilliant colours of many flowers have evolved over millions of years to make sure that tiny grains of pollen are carried from one plant to another. Pollen grains have to travel from the anthers to the stigma (pp. 16-17) for fertilization to occur and for seeds to be produced. Some plants are able to pollinate themselves (self-pollination), but most rely on receiving pollen from another plant of the same species (cross-pollination). Pollen may be dispersed by wind or by water, but the most important pollinators are insects. Plants entice insects to their flowers by their bright colours, and by food in the form of nectar. While the visiting insect feeds, pollen from the anthers is pressed on to its body, often at a particular place such as on the back, or on the head. The stigma of the flower that receives the pollen is in just the right place to collect it as the insect arrives. Some flowers are pollinated by a wide range of insects such as honeybees, bumblebees, hoverflies, and butterflies. Others are more choosy and rely so heavily on a particular pollinator that no other insect species can do the job for them. Some species of yucca, for example, are pollinated exclusively by a small moth, called the yucca moth. In return, the yucca provides the moth with food and a home.

FAMILY HOME
Worker bees bring nectar and pollen back to the hive to feed the developing young.

Pollen basket on hind leg

Honeyguide

THE FLORAL FEEDING STATION
Honeyguides (p. 12) on the flower guide the bee to the nectar. As the bees feed on the nectar, they also collect pollen in special baskets on their legs so it can be carried to the hive.

Bright yellow guide marks show bees where to land

Lower petal acts as landing platform

OPENING UP
The flower of the common toadflax is pollinated by bumblebees. When a visiting bee arrives, the throat of the flower is tightly closed. To reach the nectar at the back of the flower, the bee must open up the flower by pushing forward.

Nectar tube

CLIMBING IN
As the bumblebee climbs over the hump that seals the flower's throat and crawls inside in search of the nectar, it brushes against the anthers inside the top of the flower. These dust its back with pollen.

FEEDING TIME
As the bee feeds on the flower's nectar, any pollen it is already carrying is transferred from its back to the stigma, and the flower is pollinated.

The real thing!

POLLEN GRAINS

Although the largest pollen grains measure only about 0.2 mm across, they have extraordinarily intricate shapes. When a pollen grain lands on the stigma of a plant of the same species, it grows a fine tube down the style (p. 17) until it reaches the ovule (p. 30).

Pollen grains magnified many times to show variety of shape.

Female impersonators

Some orchids use a clever trick to ensure that they are pollinated. Each flower looks and smells like a female fly, wasp, or bee. The impersonation is so convincing that the male tries to mate with the flower. When this happens, pollen sticks to the bee's body, and when the insect eventually flies off, the pollen is carried to the next flower.

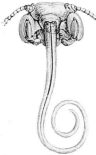

Flowers of the fly orchid

Long proboscis

BUTTERFLY POLLINATION

Butterflies are also important pollinators but, unlike bees, they do not feed on the pollen and so do not actively collect it. Instead, when they land on a flower to feed on the nectar, pollen from the anthers sticks to their bodies, ready to be carried to the next flower. Because butterflies have a highly developed sense of smell, butterfly-pollinated flowers are often scented. Many flower in late summer when butterflies are most abundant.

Proboscis sucks up nectar

Short proboscis

DRINKING STRAWS

Butterflies and moths suck up nectar through the proboscis, which is hollow like a drinking straw. The proboscis may vary in length from a fraction of a millimetre to 30 cm (1 ft). When resting, it is coiled up under the butterfly's head.

Pollen from anthers sticks to butterfly's body

Marjoram

Strange pollinators

Many flowers are pollinated by bees and butterflies (p. 22), but some plant species depend on quite different creatures for pollination. Some are pollinated by the sort of flies that are attracted by the smell of decay. Others rely on birds, which are attracted to the flowers by bright colours and the sweet smell of nectar. Many plants are highly adapted for specific pollinators. The list of these species includes not only insects and birds, but also bats, mice, possums, and even slugs.

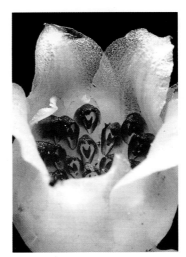

POLLINATION UNDERGROUND
Some orchids in Australia grow and flower underground, where they live on the decaying remains of other plants. The picture on the left shows the flower of one of these species. These flowers are most probably pollinated by soil-dwelling creatures, although it is not yet known exactly which one.

Hairs on petals attract insects

Flowers are lilac at first, but turn red as they open

Pink bracts attract birds

Shiny surface

Cultivated fly-pollinated orchid

A LURE FOR FLIES
Bees are attracted to flowers that have a sweet smell. Many flies, on the other hand, are attracted by the smell of decaying flesh. For this reason, many flowers that rely on flies for pollination have a putrid odour. Some flowers, such as this orchid, have hairs on the surface of their petals to give them an animal-like feel. The shiny surface also attracts flies.

Flowers appear amongst bracts

Urn plant

THE RED SIGNAL
Plants that are pollinated by birds often have red or pink petals or flower heads. Birds have excellent colour vision, and a bright red flower, which also produces nectar, readily attracts them. Because this urn plant lives high up on trees (p. 46), it needs to be conspicuous to attract the attention of the bird pollinators. Most insects, apart from some butterflies, cannot see red, so it is an unusual colour for insect-pollinated flowers.

A BRUSH FOR BIRDS

Most species of hibiscus are pollinated by hummingbirds.
A hummingbird hovers in front of the flower and inserts
its long beak deep inside to reach the nectar. As it feeds,
the anthers brush pollen on to its head, while the stigma,
also brushing its head, collects pollen from another
flower. The flower shown here is in an upright position.
In its natural state it would normally be horizontal.

*Brush-like
anthers*

Hibiscus flower

Yellow
calla lily

BIZARRE BEAUTY

The yellow calla lily, is pollinated by
insects called fungus gnats. Its separate
male and female flowers grow on a
central spike, or spadix, and are enveloped by a bright yellow bract,
called a spathe. The insects, carrying
pollen from the male flowers of
other plants, crawl to the base of
the spathe, where they become
trapped by downward-pointing
hairs. As they move around,
they pollinate the female
flowers. The hairs then
wither, and as the insects
crawl out they are dus-
ted with pollen from
the mature male
flowers, ready
to move on to
the next
plant.

*Bright yellow spathe
envelops flowers
on spadix*

POSSUM POLLINATION

The Australian honey possum is a
tiny marsupial which lives
entirely on the pollen and nectar
of flowers like this banksia. It
collects its unusual food with its
long snout and brush-like tongue.
Apart from the possum, the only
other mammals to pollinate
flowers are rodents and bats.

*"Window"
cells let in
light*

*Flies fall down this
hollow tube and are
trapped by downward-
pointing hairs*

*Trapped flies try to
escape by flying up
towards the light
and become covered
with pollen*

*Landing
flap*

TAKING PRISONERS

This weirdly shaped flower is
produced by a South American
creeper. It lures flies by its smell
of rotting fish. The flies enter the
flower and are imprisoned within
it overnight. When the flower
begins to wither, the flies - now
covered in pollen - can escape.

Brazilian
birthwort

Colourful lobe attracts flies

From flower to fruit

AFTER A FLOWER HAS BEEN POLLINATED (pp. 22-23), it normally has to be fertilized before it will produce seeds and fruits. When a pollen grain lands on the stigma of a flower of the same species, it germinates to produce a pollen tube. This grows through the stigma and down the style to fertilize the ovule (p. 17). One of the two male cells in the pollen grain fuses with the egg cell in the ovule. This fused cell then divides to form an embryo plant. A food reserve, or endosperm, is formed around the embryo plant by the second male cell, which fuses with two other cells in the ovule. The embryo plant, together with its food store and protective coat, or testa, is known as the seed. The fruit is usually formed from the ovary, the protective structure around the seeds. However, in some cases, other parts of the flower protect both the seed and the ovary. In the rose, the "pips" inside the rose hip are technically the fruits, and the fleshy outer part is known as the receptacle. The fruit often helps in seed dispersal. The most obvious fruits are sweet, juicy, and brightly coloured, tempting animals to eat them and so disperse the seeds (p. 28). However, the fruits of some plants include dry pods, which flick the seeds in all directions (p. 29), or fluffy plumes that help carry the seeds and fruits high on the breeze (p. 30).

WINTER FEAST
Fruits are an important source of winter food for many animals. Here a redwing feasts on fallen apples and may help to spread the apples' seeds.

Sepals protect developing bud

Receptacle containing ovaries

EARLY DAYS
Even before the rose comes into flower, the beginnings of the rose hip can be clearly seen. The top of the stem, to which the flower parts are attached, is swollen and globular, as this bud shows. The female parts of the flower, the ovaries and ovules, are inside this swollen area, or receptacle.

THE ROSE IN BLOOM
As the bud opens, the flower gives off its sweet scent, which attracts bees for pollination (pp. 22-23). Once the flower has been pollinated and the ovules fertilized, the receptacle begins to swell.

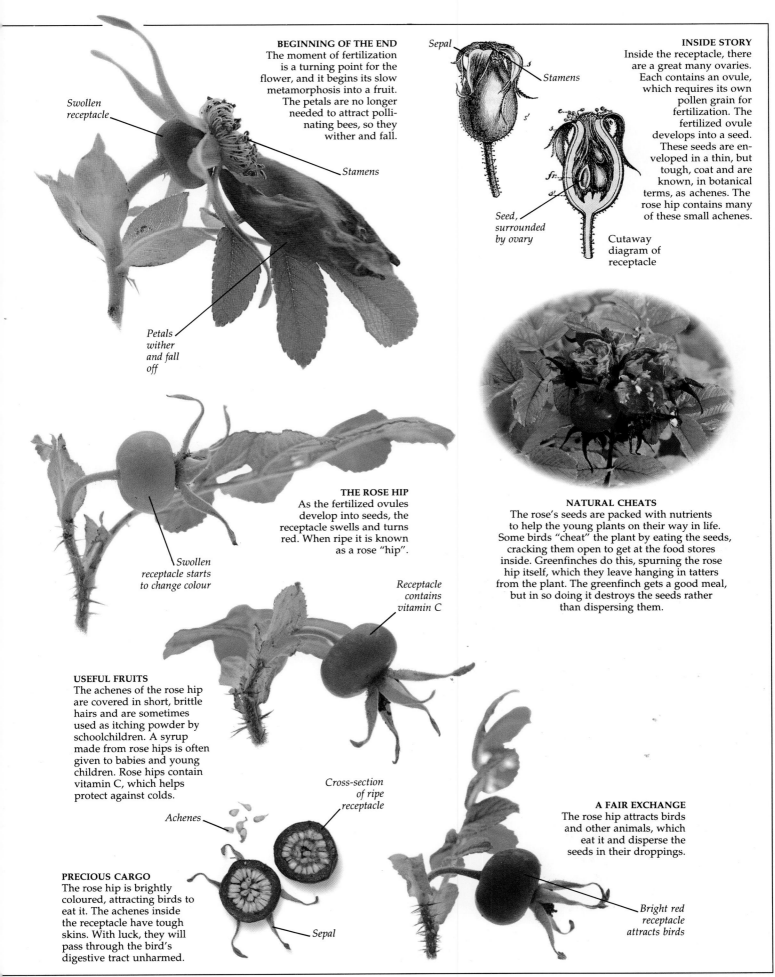

BEGINNING OF THE END
The moment of fertilization is a turning point for the flower, and it begins its slow metamorphosis into a fruit. The petals are no longer needed to attract pollinating bees, so they wither and fall.

Swollen receptacle

Stamens

Petals wither and fall off

Sepal

Stamens

Seed, surrounded by ovary

Cutaway diagram of receptacle

INSIDE STORY
Inside the receptacle, there are a great many ovaries. Each contains an ovule, which requires its own pollen grain for fertilization. The fertilized ovule develops into a seed. These seeds are enveloped in a thin, but tough, coat and are known, in botanical terms, as achenes. The rose hip contains many of these small achenes.

Swollen receptacle starts to change colour

THE ROSE HIP
As the fertilized ovules develop into seeds, the receptacle swells and turns red. When ripe it is known as a rose "hip".

NATURAL CHEATS
The rose's seeds are packed with nutrients to help the young plants on their way in life. Some birds "cheat" the plant by eating the seeds, cracking them open to get at the food stores inside. Greenfinches do this, spurning the rose hip itself, which they leave hanging in tatters from the plant. The greenfinch gets a good meal, but in so doing it destroys the seeds rather than dispersing them.

Receptacle contains vitamin C

USEFUL FRUITS
The achenes of the rose hip are covered in short, brittle hairs and are sometimes used as itching powder by schoolchildren. A syrup made from rose hips is often given to babies and young children. Rose hips contain vitamin C, which helps protect against colds.

Achenes

Cross-section of ripe receptacle

A FAIR EXCHANGE
The rose hip attracts birds and other animals, which eat it and disperse the seeds in their droppings.

PRECIOUS CARGO
The rose hip is brightly coloured, attracting birds to eat it. The achenes inside the receptacle have tough skins. With luck, they will pass through the bird's digestive tract unharmed.

Sepal

Bright red receptacle attracts birds

How seeds are spread

Agrimony

AS ALL GARDENERS KNOW, a patch of bare soil never stays bare for long. Within days, seedlings start to spring up, and if the conditions are right, they eventually cover the ground. Even if the earth is sterilized by heating, so that all the seeds are killed, more somehow arrive and germinate. Plants have evolved some very effective ways of spreading their seeds. In certain plants, exploding seed pods fling the seeds into the air. Others have flying or floating seeds, or fruits, which are carried far and wide by the wind and by water currents. Animals also play their part. Many plants have fruits with hooks that stick to fur. The seeds of some species develop inside tasty berries. Although the berries are eaten by animals and birds, the seeds pass through these creatures unharmed and fall to the ground where they germinate.

Fruits have hooks

Each fruit has many tiny hooks

Lesser burdock

Lotus seed heads

Seed held in cup

Dried lotus seed head from above

Lotuses growing in ancient Egypt

HITCHING A LIFT
The best way to find out which seeds are dispersed by animals is to go for a walk through rough grassland. You will probably return home with the fruits of a number of different plants stuck to your clothes. Known as "burrs", these fruits have hooks and spines which cling to the fur and wool of passing animals. When the burrs are rubbed or scratched off, their seeds fall to the ground and germinate.

Burrs cling to the fur on this dog's back

WASHED AWAY
The lotus is a water plant that produces its seeds in a flattened head. When the seeds are ripe, they fall on to the water's surface and float away. Lotus seeds can be extraordinarily long-lived. Some have been known to germinate more than 200 years after they were shed.

Some plants disperse their seeds with natural catapults. These work by suddenly releasing tension that builds up as the seed case grows: the seed case splits open, flinging the seeds in all directions. These catapults are triggered in a number of ways. Some, particularly the pods of pea-family plants such as vetches, burst open when the sun dries them. Others, such as the Himalayan balsam (p. 18), are triggered by movement, either the wind blowing past, or by an animal brushing against the plant.

Closed seed pod

When touched, the seed case curls up suddenly and the seeds are flicked out

Unexploded seed pod

Seeds of meadow cranesbill are catapulted out

Himalayan balsam flower

Tiny, light seeds

Columbine

BLOWING IN THE WIND

Seeds that are dispersed by the wind must be small and light if they are to be carried any distance by the breeze. When the wind shakes the seed heads of plants such as the opium poppy, and columbine, the seeds are scattered just a short distance from the parent plant. When a thistle seed head catches the wind, its fruits (containing the seeds) can be swept high into the air, and be carried much farther.

Pods of tufted vetch snap open when dry

Intact pod

Fruits have parachutes so they can be carried by the wind

Seeds are sprinkled

Opium poppy

SHUNNING THE LIGHT

The ivy-leaved toad-flax grows on walls and rock faces. As its seeds ripen, the stems carrying the seed heads grow away from the light, pushing the seeds into cracks and crevices. This ensures that they have somewhere suitable to germinate.

Creeping thistle

29

Borne on the wind

ACCORDING TO TRADITION, if you blow on a dandelion's seed head, the number of puffs needed to blow away all the seeds will tell you the time of day. Whether or not this is true, it is a custom that certainly helps the plant to spread. The seeds of the dandelion are encased in tiny fruits and have their own special feathery parachutes to help them float through the air. If you blow on them, you may be starting the seeds on a journey that takes them high up and far away. The dandelion's flower, like that of the sunflower (p. 21), is actually a composite flower head made up of many tiny florets. Each of the florets produces a single fruit. Like the dandelion, many other composite plants, such as hawkweeds, ragworts, and thistles, rely on the wind to disperse their seeds. The fruits of some of these have parachutes; others have fine hairs that stick out in all directions to form a feathery ball. Many of these plants are troublesome weeds because they quickly colonize bare soil in gardens and on farmland.

Dandelion's tiny fruits float away on the breeze

1 OPENING TIME
The dandelion's flower opens in the morning and closes in the afternoon or when it rains. The plant's name comes from the French *dent de lion*, meaning lion's tooth, which describes the jagged edges of the leaves.

Flower closes before seeds form

Flower head open, waiting to be pollinated by a passing insect

2 THE SEEDS START TO FORM
After opening and closing for a number of days, during which time it may be pollinated, the flower finally closes, and seed formation begins. Gradually the yellow petals wither away, and the "pappus", which is the name given to the small circle of hairs attached to the top of each fruit, starts to grow longer. This is the beginning of the parachute.

Bracts protect developing seed head

*Seed head
opens when
parachutes
are formed*

*Bracts
fold
back*

3 OPENING OUT

The seed head begins to open only when the weather is dry. At first, the parachutes are squashed together, but as the bracts around the edge of the seed head fold back, the parachutes begin to expand.

4 READY TO GO

If the air is still, the fruits may spend several days attached to the seed head. This is a dangerous time for them, because seed-eating birds like goldfinches are likely to peck them off and eat them.

*Fully opened
seed head*

*Parachutes attached
to tiny fruits*

5 LIFT OFF

A slight breeze is all that is needed to lift the parachutes into the air. They may fall close by, but if there is enough updraught they can be carried for long distances. When a fruit lands, it no longer needs the parachute that has carried it on its journey, and this breaks off. Over the winter the seed sinks into the soil, waiting for the spring when it begins to germinate.

Spreading without seeds

Piggyback plant

PLANTS CAN REPRODUCE in two quite different ways. As well as reproducing by means of seeds, they can sometimes also turn small pieces of themselves into new plants. This is known as vegetative reproduction. When a plant reproduces in this way, the young plantlets are genetically identical to the parent. This is quite different from reproduction with seeds, which produce seedlings that are all slightly different from their parents. Vegetative reproduction is very useful for farmers and gardeners. It means that they can multiply a plant that has attractive flowers or tasty fruit, knowing that each young plant will have exactly the characteristics they want. Some of the oldest plants in the world are perpetuated by vegetative reproduction. These are creosote plant "clones" in California. Each clone is created when a single creosote plant begins to spread by producing young plants connected to it. The original creosote plant at the centre, which began life about 10,000 years ago, is now long dead, but its clones are still alive and spreading today.

THE PIGGYBACK PLANT
The piggyback plant has an unusual way of reproducing. Tiny new plantlets grow at the base of the older leaves and look as though they are having a piggyback ride.

Creeping buttercup

Parent plant

CREEPING STEMS
Some plants, such as the creeping buttercup, spread by means of stolons, which are leafy stems that grow along the ground. When the stolons reach a certain length, a new, young plant develops from a bud at the leaf node (p. 9) and the stolon eventually withers away completely.

Fallen plantlets

Strawberry plant

Parent plant

Stolon, or runner

Bud at leaf node

Chandelier plant

PLANTLETS AT LEAF TIPS
Kalanchoes are succulents (p. 53) many of which reproduce by developing tiny plantlets along the edges of their leaves. Others, like this chandelier plant, have them just at the tips. When a plantlet is mature, it falls off the parent plant and takes root in the soil beneath.

STRAWBERRY RUNNERS
After they have fruited, strawberry plants produce long stolons known as runners, which spread out over the ground. Strawberry growers wait until the young plants have rooted and then cut the runners. The new plants can be transplanted to make a new strawberry bed.

A MYTH EXPLODED
The famous tumbleweed of the North American prairies is uprooted by strong winds after it has flowered and is often blown far away from the place where it grew. Because it is dead, the plant cannot put down roots once it comes to a halt, as is often supposed. Instead, it spreads by seeds. The plant scatters them as it tumbles along the ground.

Iris

RHIZOMES
A rhizome is a usually horizontal stem produced by a perennial plant, either underground or on the surface. As the rhizome spreads, it occasionally divides, producing roots, stems, and leaves. The oldest part of the rhizome may die away so that these new shoots form separate plants.

Iris rhizome

Tuber of Jerusalem artichoke

TUBERS
Tubers are swollen underground stems. They store food to produce new plants and also to help the parent plant to survive in adverse conditions. When gardeners and farmers lift tuber crops like potatoes, they have to be careful to dig up every one. If even part of the potato is left in the ground, it will sprout to produce a new plant the following spring.

Tuber of potato

Stolon

Young plant forming at tip of stolon

Young plant grows from a bud at the leaf node

Runner

Tulip bulb

BULBS
A bulb consists of a bud surrounded by short and very swollen leaves, with flattened underground stems. Some bulbs, such as the tulip, produce one or more new bulbs around its base every year. These can be broken off the parent bulb to form new plants.

New bulbs form around the base of the old bulb

LEAVES THAT TAKE ROOT
Plants that live in dry places often have fleshy leaves that are full of water. If these leaves are broken off, they can survive for a long time, because they do not dry out as quickly as normal, thin leaves. While they are lying on the ground, many of them can put down roots and develop into new plants.

Crassula nealana

BULBS ABOVE AND BELOW GROUND
This species of onion has both bulbs and bulbils, small bulb-like structures that form above ground in place of flowers.

Bulbils may fall to the ground and take root

Fleshy leaves can root themselves

Top of plant

Bulb underground

Sedum rubrotinctum

Allium paradoxum

Living leaves

Water plants often have feathery leaves to allow the water to flow past without damaging them

Leaves are so varied that botanists have invented a whole new language to describe their shapes and the way they are fixed to plants. One reason for all this variety is that each species of plant has its own special problems in harvesting sunlight (pp. 14-15). A plant living on the gloomy floor of a rainforest, for example, may need large leaves to catch enough light. A plant growing on a cliff top has no shortage of light, but is lashed by strong winds. So it needs small, strong leaves if it is to survive. Some plants have more than one type of leaf. This is most marked in plants which start their lives underwater but then flower above it. One example of this is the water crowfoot. Its submerged leaves are fine and feathery, to let water flow past without tearing them, while the upper leaves are flat and broad so that they float on the surface.

CHANGING COLOUR
The leaves of herb Robert change from green to crimson as autumn approaches, or in very dry weather.

Older leaves

DIFFERENT SHAPES
This eucalyptus tree has leaves of two totally different shapes. The leaves of the young stems are round, like coins, and each one completely encircles the branch. The leaves on the older parts of the stems have stalks and are shaped like short straps.

PARALLEL VEINS *left*
The leaves of plants such as grasses, orchids, and lilies have parallel veins (p. 9). These strap-like leaves are from a member of the lily family.

FURRY LEAVES
Some leaves have "fur" which helps to reduce water loss. These leaves are from a cultivated pyrethrum which is grown in gardens.

Young leaves

Leaf supported by strong ribs

FACING THE WIND
Wild asparagus lives on windy coasts. Instead of true leaves it has feathery, green, leaf-like stems, called cladodes, which are able to withstand gales. Large, fleshy leaves would be torn to pieces.

WATERSIDE GIANTS
Gunneras grow on riverbanks in tropical forests, but are sometimes found beside water in warmer parts of temperate countries. Their leaves can be enormous - as much as 2 m (6 ft) in diameter.

Asparagus

Underside of a section of a gunnera leaf

Leaflet

Leaves that are
made up of a number
of individual leaflets
are called compound
leaves

SLASHED LEAVES
The Swiss cheese
plant grows in tropical
forests, clinging to trees
for support. It probably
gets its name from its unusual
leaves. With all their slashes
and perforations they are
reminiscent of some types of
very holey Swiss cheese.

Leaves without
leaflets are
known as
simple
leaves

*Waxy
upper
surface*

*Slashes appear as
the leaf grows older*

Peltate leaves are
circular, with the
stalk inserted in the
middle

EVERGREEN LEAVES *left*
Evergreen plants do not
lose their leaves in the
winter, so their leaves
need to be tough to
survive several years
in the wind, sun, and
rain. Rhododendron
leaves have a waxy
upper surface to
prevent them from
drying out, and
some species also
have felt-like down
on their undersides
to retain moisture
and ward off insects.

Joseph's
coat

*Some
varieties
have red
undersides*

Rhododendron
leaves

*Downy
underside*

Lungwort

**MULTICOLOURED
LEAVES**
Variegated leaves are
often found in garden plants. The
lungwort gets its name from its spotty leaves
which give it the appearance of a human lung.
In times gone by, it was also used as a cure for lung diseases.

35

Self-defence

Pᴌᴀɴᴛꜱ ᴄᴀɴɴᴏᴛ ʀᴜɴ ᴀᴡᴀʏ from their enemies in the same way as animals, so they have evolved special weapons and armour to protect themselves. The main enemies of most plants are the animals that feed on them. These range in size from tiny insects, which suck sap, or chew their way through leaves, to large mammals, which eat entire plants. To keep the smallest enemies at bay, many plants have a mat of fine hairs on the surface of their leaves. Larger animals are deterred by means of special weaponry which includes spines, thorns, and stings. As a final defence, many plants have chemicals in their cells which make them unpleasant to eat. Once an animal has tasted the plant, it is unlikely to want to repeat the experience.

Thorns grow in pairs

Hole through which ants enter thorn

Dried acacia twig

Gall

Ant

Barbs along edge of leaf

Long, sharp spines

Small, fleshy leaves

This nettle sting has been magnified many times to show the sharp tip

ANTS ON GUARD
Some acacia trees rely on ants to keep away browsing animals. In return for food and lodgings the ants ferociously attack any animal which tries to feed on the tree's leaves. The ants eat the sweet-tasting pith of the thorns and make them hollow. They also feed from a row of nectaries at the base of each leaf. The Bull horn acacia even produces little knobs of protein and fat at the tip of each leaflet, which ensures that the ants protect the whole leaf.

CHEMICAL WARFARE
The stings of the nettle are like hypodermic syringes. The walls of the sting cell are impregnated with a glass-like substance called silica (p. 7). When an animal brushes past the nettle, the stings puncture its skin and release a cocktail of chemicals which causes a painful irritation. On future encounters animals remember the sting and avoid the nettle.

RUNNING INTO TROUBLE
Screw pines are tropical plants that have tough, sword-shaped leaves. These have rows of vicious barbs, not only along their edges, but also along their midribs. The barbs point away from the plant, so any animal trying to get near it runs the risk of being impaled, as it pushes forward.

Alluaudia

Barbs along midrib

Nettle

PROTECTED LEAVES
Plants that live in hot, dry climates need to defend themselves, because their leaves are a tempting source of food and water for animals. Many of them, such as cacti, do this with spines (pp. 52-53). This plant from Madagascar has spines that are longer than its leaves, making it very hard for large animals to reach them.

Leaf of screw pine

Pairs of straight thorns keep animals away

TANGLED IN A TRAP

Thorns on flexible stems snag passing animals and give them a painful lesson, teaching them not to get too close again. Thorns can either be straight, as on this rose, or they can be curved, which makes them dig in when they are pulled. Some plants have thorns pointing in both directions along their stems. If an animal gets tangled in the plant, the thorns catch no matter which way it pulls.

Thistle in flower

Unopened flower head protected by spiny bracts

Woolly thistle

ARMOURED FLOWERS

Thistles are extremely successful plants, partly because they have an effective seed dispersal system (p. 27) and partly because they are very well defended. Most thistles have spines on their stems as well as on their leaves. They also have spiny flaps, known as bracts, which protect their developing flower heads. The spines keep most animals away, although they do not deter sap-sucking insects such as aphids, which often feed in large numbers on thistles.

Spiny bracts protect the developing flower head

DEATH BY DROWNING

Pairs of leaves on the stem of the teasel meet to form little cups which fill with water after rain. Each cup acts like a moat to protect the plant. Snails and insects try to climb the plant to feed on its young leaves but, faced with the water, they either turn back or fall into the moat and drown.

Young, spiny flower head

Teasel

Holly leaves

Insects drowned in moat formed at the point where the paired leaves meet

EXTRA WEAPONRY

Holly leaves are not only very leathery, they also have tough spines all around their edges. Compared to the leaves of deciduous trees, which lose their leaves every autumn, they suffer very little from animal attack. These leaves are from a variety of holly which has been cultivated to produce extra spines. On holly trees, the lowest leaves are usually the spiniest. Those nearest the top may have no spines at all, as they are in less danger of being eaten.

Spines protect stem

Creepers and climbers

Wherever there is moisture and warmth, plants struggle against each other for light. The tallest plant usually gets the greatest share, but it also has to spend the most energy in growing a strong stem, or a tree trunk, to hold up its leaves. But there are some plants - epiphytes (pp. 46-47) and climbers - which take a short cut to the top. They take advantage of other plants and even buildings to get a place in the light with much less effort. Epiphytes may grow on the trunks or upper branches of trees and are lifted up with them as they grow. These plants do not have roots on the ground and are able to absorb all the water they need from the air and rainwater. Climbers need supports. Some twine themselves around a plant, while others put out touch-sensitive feelers, or tendrils, which curl around the support when they come into contact with it. A third group of climbers raise themselves by means of stiff side branches, prickles, roots, or hairs.

GROWING IN A SPIRAL
Plants which grow in a spiral twist in a set direction. Runner bean plants always twist in a clockwise direction, a detail noticed by the artist who made this 16th-century woodcut of a bean plant climbing up a stick.

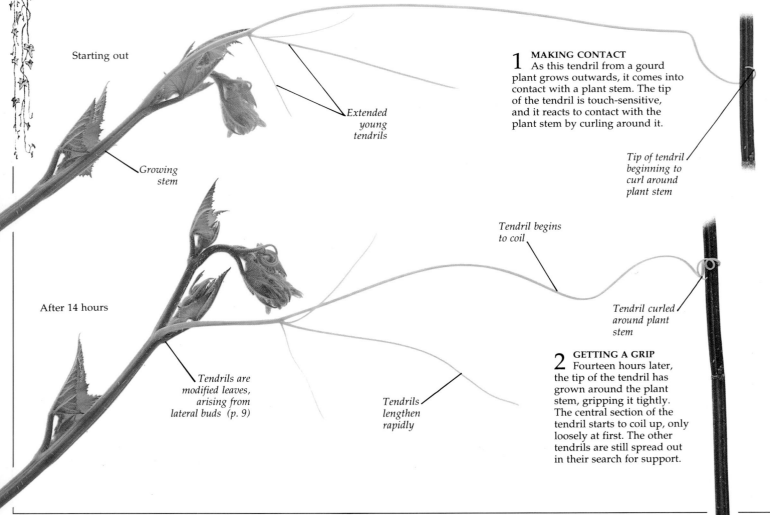

Starting out

Extended young tendrils

Growing stem

After 14 hours

Tendrils are modified leaves, arising from lateral buds (p. 9)

Tendrils lengthen rapidly

1 MAKING CONTACT
As this tendril from a gourd plant grows outwards, it comes into contact with a plant stem. The tip of the tendril is touch-sensitive, and it reacts to contact with the plant stem by curling around it.

Tip of tendril beginning to curl around plant stem

Tendril begins to coil

Tendril curled around plant stem

2 GETTING A GRIP
Fourteen hours later, the tip of the tendril has grown around the plant stem, gripping it tightly. The central section of the tendril starts to coil up, only loosely at first. The other tendrils are still spread out in their search for support.

Young leaf

Next bunch of tendrils

As the tendril coils, it shortens and pulls the plant towards the support

After 24 hours

3 COILING UP
Twenty-four hours after making contact, the tendril has now formed a double coil. This makes it shorten, so the plant is pulled towards the support. Another bunch of tendrils is now starting to appear farther along the growing stem.

Boston ivy growing on a tree

Extended tendril still searching for a support

Next tendril makes contact higher up this plant stem

Sucker-like pads

Tightly coiled tendril

STICKING TO A SURFACE
Many plants related to the grape vine have tendrils with small, sucker-like pads at the tip. These stick to other plants or walls. The tendrils then coil up to hold the plant to the surface.

Old tendril coils up

After 48 hours

Adventitious roots

CLIMBING WITH ROOTS
Ivy holds on to trees and vertical surfaces by means of short adventitious roots. These anchor themselves in any crevices, supporting the plant as it climbs upwards. Although ivy may look like a parasite (pp. 44-45) it is not. It uses other plants only for support, but unfortunately sometimes kills them in the process by smothering them with its leaves.

Ivy

Ivy climbing over a statue

4 MAKING FAST
Forty-eight hours after making contact, the tendril has now coiled up tightly like a spring, and the plant is securely supported. If the wind blows, the coils will allow the tendril to stretch rather than being broken.

Meat eaters

ALTHOUGH MAN-EATING PLANTS belong to
the world of fiction, there are many plants
that eat insects and other small animals.
These meat-eating, or carnivorous, plants
fall into two groups. Some species, such as
the Venus flytrap (pp. 42-43), have active
traps, with moving parts that catch their
prey. Other species have inactive traps with
no moving parts. They simply attract their
victims with a scent reminiscent of food,
and then catch them on a sticky surface or
drown them in a pool of fluid. The victims of
carnivorous plants are mostly insects. Once an
insect has been caught, it is slowly dissolved by
digestive fluids produced by the plant. After many
days, all that is left is the insect's exoskeleton - the
hard outer casing of the body. The rest of the
insect has been absorbed by the plant. Carnivorous
plants can make food from sunlight like ordinary
plants. The insects they catch are simply used as a
dietary supplement - they are the plants' equivalent
of vitamin tablets. Many plants need this extra source
of food because they grow in waterlogged ground
where the soil is deficient in
nitrates and other essential
nutrients.

SPECIALIZED LEAVES
All the animal traps shown on
these two pages are modified
leaves. The leaves of the
Portuguese sundew are so sticky
that they used to be hung up
indoors to catch flies.

*Flower of
Cape sundew*

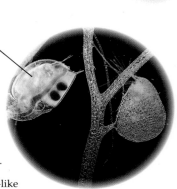
*Lid keeps
out rain*

Rim

FATAL ATTRACTION
This colourful nepenthes
pitcher lures passing insects.

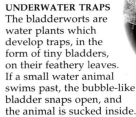
*Water flea
trapped by a
bladderwort*

UNDERWATER TRAPS
The bladderworts are
water plants which
develop traps, in the
form of tiny bladders,
on their feathery leaves.
If a small water animal
swims past, the bubble-like
bladder snaps open, and
the animal is sucked inside.

THE STICKY SUNDEWS
The leaves of sundews are covered
in hairs which produce drop-
lets of sticky "glue". When an
insect lands on one of the
leaves, it sticks to the
hairs, which then fold
over, trapping it.

Magnification of
a fly trapped
by hairs on
sundew leaf

Cape
sundew

LYING IN WAIT
Butterworts have circles of flat, sticky
leaves. These plants may not look very
threatening, but when an insect lands
on a leaf, it becomes glued to the
surface and eventually dies.
The edges of the leaf very
gradually curl inwards, and
the insect is digested. There
are about 50 species of
butterwort, most of which
grow in marshy places.

*Leaf covered with
short, sticky hairs*

Butterwort

Hanging
nepenthes
pitcher

An 18th-century engraving
of hanging nepenthes
pitcher plants

*Leaf of hanging
pitcher plant*

DEATH IN THE SWAMPS
American pitcher plants catch
their food in the same way as the
hanging pitcher plants, but instead of
hanging from leaves, their pitchers grow up
from the ground. The inside of each pitcher
is lined with scales of wax, so the insects
are unable to hang on to the sides as they
tumble towards the liquid below. Once in
the liquid, the scales prevent them from
climbing back up the sides of
the pitcher.

*American pitcher
plant has a
frilly rim*

COBRA LILY *below*
The California pitcher
plant, or cobra lily,
looks similar to a snake,
rearing up and flicking out its
tongue. Insects, lured by nectar,
enter the plant through the
"mouth". Once inside the pitcher,
they are confused by light shining
down through small "windows" at
the top. In the attempt to escape, the
insects fly continually towards the light,
but eventually become exhausted, drop-
ping into the liquid and drowning.

*Rim where nectar
is produced*

HANGING PITCHER PLANT
The traps of hanging pitcher
plants grow at the ends of their
leaves. Each one is like a jug and
has a lid to keep out the rain.
Insects are lured to the pitcher
by its bright colour and by nectar
which is produced around the
rim. The surface of the rim is
slippery, so when insects try
to settle on it, they lose their
footing, fall inside, and drown
in the fluid at the bottom.
Hanging pitcher plants
grow in Southeast Asia.
The largest pitchers are
up to 35 cm (14 in) deep
and hold a cupful
of fluid.

"Windows"

*These insects are
being slowly
digested in the
fluid that collects
at the bottom of
the pitcher*

*Entrance to
pitcher
"mouth"*

Vertical cross-section
through hanging pitcher

This American
pitcher plant is
known as a parrot
pitcher plant

Cobra lily

41

Caught in a trap

To AN UNWARY INSECT, the unusual leaf tips of the Venus flytrap appear most inviting. Not only is the insect attracted by what looks like a safe landing place, it is also tempted by the promise of food in the form of nectar. But it is all a trick. As soon as the insect settles, the leaf tips spring to life with lightning speed. Within a second, the hapless insect finds itself trapped, as the two halves of the leaf snap shut. There is a second, slower phase of closure after the plant has tested what it has caught using sensory glands on the surface of its lobes. If the prey contains protein, the trap closes fully, and digestion begins. The traps of the Venus flytrap are formed by two kidney-shaped lobes at the tip of the leaf, with a hinge formed by the midrib. The whole of the leaf is green and therefore able to photosynthesize (pp. 14-15). Large bristles on the upper surface of the trap work like triggers with a clever device. If just one bristle is touched, by a raindrop for example, the trap stays open. But if two or more bristles are touched in quick succession, it quickly shuts to catch its victim.

A MOST HORRIBLE TORTURE
Insects were not the only ones to be condemned to a frightful and lingering death, as this rather gruesome engraving shows.

Marginal teeth

Trigger bristle

Damselfly touches trigger bristles

Damselfly is caught in closing trap

Midrib of leaf

Kidney-shaped leaf tip

1 THE TRAP IS TRIGGERED
A damselfly lands on the trap and touches the trigger bristles on the trap's upper surface. Initially, special cells in the hinge, called "motor" cells, are filled with liquid. As soon as the triggers are fired, this liquid rushes out of the motor cells, making them collapse. This causes the trap to spring shut. The damselfly either does not notice this movement, or reacts too slowly.

2 CLOSING UP
After about one-fifth of a second, the sides of the trap are already closing over their victim. Because the marginal teeth point slightly outwards, they help to make sure that the insect does not fall out as the trap shuts. Even if it has sensed danger, it is now too late for the damselfly to make its escape.

Lower part of leaf

Open trap

After one-fifth of a second

An early
19th-century
_____ of
_____ nus
_____ by
_____ te, who
_____ ed the
plants kept by
the Empress
Josephine at
Malmaison
(p. 61)

Flower stem

Open trap

GROWING A FLYTRAP
The first living specimen of the Venus flytrap arrived in England from America in the mid 18th century. Never before had such an unusual and spectacular plant been seen live in Europe, and it aroused great curiosity among botanists. Today Venus flytraps can be grown as pot plants. Because they come from waterlogged bogs with slightly acid soil, they must never be allowed to dry out and are best planted in peat. It is important to water them with distilled water, because tap water often contains dissolved minerals that will reduce the plant's chances of survival. Venus flytraps do produce clusters of white flowers, but this does not often happen with indoor specimens, especially if they are frequently fed with insects.

A WATERY HABITAT
Venus flytraps come from the bogs of North Carolina in the eastern United States. Each plant grows from a small rhizome, and produces several traps. Each trap can catch about three insects before it withers.

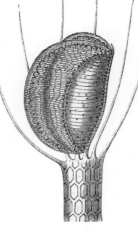

FLOATING TRAPS
This waterwheel plant is a small water plant that belongs to the same family of plants as the Venus flytrap and the sundews. Its leaves end in small traps that catch tiny water animals. They can close in one-fiftieth of a second.

Marginal teeth closing around insect

Marginal teeth form a cage around the damselfly

Trap almost closed

3 COMING TOGETHER
After two-fifths of a second, the marginal teeth have almost met. They are arranged alternately, so that they do not crash into each other as the trap closes. Meanwhile, inside the trap, the trigger bristles fold back. This ensures that they are not damaged and will be able to work again when the trap reopens.

After two-fifths of a second

4 ALL EXITS SEALED
When the trap shuts, its sides remain at a slight angle to each other. At this stage very small insects can climb out between the marginal teeth, but the damselfly is too big and is securely held in. The trap would be wasted on small insects, as it can only digest two or three insects before it becomes ineffective. After 30 minutes the sides of the trap will close fully and the plant will begin to digest its prisoner.

5 DIGESTION
Special glands inside the trap secrete acid and substances called enzymes, which will slowly digest all the soft parts of the insect's body. These glands later absorb the digested insect. It will take about two weeks for the damselfly to be fully digested, and for the trap to be ready for another meal. When the trap re-opens, the insect's hard exoskeleton, which includes the wings, will blow away.

Parasitic plants

Giant rafflesia flower

PARASITIC PLANTS are cheats. Rather than making their own food using the energy from sunlight, they have developed a means of stealing the food made by other plants, known as host plants. Because they do not need sunlight, many parasitic plants spend most of their lives hidden from sight. They attach themselves to the stems or roots of their host plants by means of suckers, known as haustoria. The haustoria penetrate the host's food channels and absorb the sugars and minerals which the parasitic plant needs to live. The world of parasitic plants is a complicated one. Some plants, such as mistletoe and the eyebrights, are only partly parasitic and are known as "hemiparasites". These plants have green leaves and so they can use the sun's energy to make some food themselves.

Giant sepals unfold as flower opens

THE STINKING GIANT
The world's heaviest flower is a species of rafflesia, a parasite which lives on the roots of vines in the jungles of Southeast Asia. Each flower weighs nearly 7 kg (15 lb) and reaches up to 1 m (3 ft) in diameter. The flower fills the air with a putrid smell which attracts pollinating flies. This plant is the largest of 50 species, all of them completely parasitic.

Sepals are thick and fleshy

Dodder flowers

Dodder stem twisting around stem of host plant

MAKING A BREAK-IN
Dodder stems spread over their hosts looking like lengths of tangled string. These stems develop haustoria that penetrate their host's food channels. Young dodders have roots to help them become established, but as they grow, the roots wither away.

Dodder flowers   Haustoria penetrating stem of host

Plant passengers

Not all plants that live on others are parasites (pp. 44-45). In fact, many more of them are simply passengers that grow on larger plants, such as trees, without causing them any harm. Such plants are described as "epiphytic" and many of them can get all the water they need simply by absorbing it from the air, or by collecting it in structures formed for the purpose. They collect minerals by extracting them from trickling rainwater and plant debris. Being an epiphyte gives a small plant a chance to collect a lot of light without the need of tall stems. So successful is this way of life that few trees are without their passengers. In cool parts of the world, epiphytes are usually small, simple plants, such as algae, lichens, and mosses. But in moist regions close to the equator, they are much larger. As well as the plants that spend their entire lives up in the trees, there are others that start or end their lives in this way. Some creeping plants, known as stranglers, germinate on trees and then become rooted in the soil. Others climb up on to plants but then their roots wither away, leaving them perched high up near the light.

These large, woody climbers, known as lianas, grow in the forests of Central America

Leaves have a special coating to reduce water loss

In the forests of Sri Lanka, epiphytic orchids grow on the trees

THE BROMELIAD'S PRIVATE POND
The bromeliads are a family of plants which includes the pineapple. Many of them grow on other plants. Instead of collecting water with long, aerial roots like orchids, they channel rainwater into a central reservoir (right) with their stiff, spiky leaves. Hairs on the leaves then absorb the water so the plant can use it. A big bromeliad holds over 5 litres (1 gallon) of water, and provides a home for water animals such as tree-frog tadpoles.

A species of
moth orchid

EPIPHYTIC ORCHIDS

There are about 18,000 species of orchid in the world. Many tropical orchids live by perching on other plants. Orchid seeds are tiny, and a single plant may produce a million of them. The wind blows the seeds of epiphytic species on to the bark of trees, where they can germinate. Each of these perching orchids has three types of aerial root, for clinging to the host, for absorbing minerals, and for extracting water from the atmosphere. Some epiphytic orchids store water and food reserves in swollen stems called pseudobulbs.

Flowers produce minute, wind-dispersed seeds

Thick, trailing aerial roots collect moisture, as well as minerals from trickling rainwater

Liana stems make a natural rope

NATURAL ROPES

Lianas are climbing plants with flexible woody stems. Sometimes they twine around each other for mutual support. If the original support dies and decays, the lianas are left suspended from the forest canopy. Other plants, called stranglers, start life above ground and then grow roots downwards. Their roots form a mesh around the trunks of trees and eventually kill the support.

Tarzan used lianas to swing from tree to tree across the jungle

Adapting to water

THE FIRST PLANTS ON EARTH evolved in water. Today, water still teems with microscopic plants that have changed little from those distant ancestors. But aquatic flowering plants have a different history. Their ancestors originally left water and evolved on land, but as time has gone by they have returned to the watery habitat. Only a few flowering plants, such as the eel-grasses, live in the sea. Far more plant species live in ponds, lakes, and rivers. Most of them are rooted to the bottom, but some have no roots and receive all the nutrients they need from the water instead of the soil. Some water plants are not often noticed because they spend all their lives underwater. Species like the water lilies, are much more obvious because their leaves float on the surface. Plants such as reeds and rushes form a group known as emergent plants. They grow up out of the water and often form thick beds at the water's edge.

HISTORIC HIDEOUT
The Pharaoh's daughter discovers Moses hidden in the bulrushes at the water's edge.

Glossy yellow flowers

LEAVING THE WATER
The greater spearwort is an example of an emergent water plant. It starts its annual cycle of growth underwater, but quickly reaches the surface. The flowers bloom about 60 cm (2 ft) above the water where they attract pollinating insects.

Greater spearwort

Spear-shaped leaves

UNDERWATER LEAVES
Fanwort has finely divided underwater leaves which are not damaged by the current.

Fanwort

Victorian engraving of papyrus growing by the Nile in Egypt

A PLANT FOR PAPER
Papyrus is a giant reed that grows up to 3 m (9 ft) high. The ancient Egyptians discovered that the pith in the middle of its stems could be used to make a material for writing on - the very first paper.

AMAZONIAN GIANT
The floating leaves of the Amazonian water lily can reach a diameter of more than 2 m (6 ft).

FLOATING ON THE SURFACE
When young, the leaves of water lilies are rolled up underwater like short tubes. In spring, the leaves reach the surface, where they open out and lie flat to form "pads". In some ponds and lakes, water lilies and other plants with floating leaves can completely cover the water's surface, robbing submerged plants of the light they need to survive. The leaves are tough and leathery so water easily runs off their surface.

Tough, waxy surface repels water

Flexible stalks attach leaves to the roots, anchored in the muddy bottom

Surviving above the snowline

THE HIGHER THE ALTITUDE at which a plant grows, the colder the temperatures it has to endure. Very low temperatures create specific problems for plant life. Thin mountain air holds little heat, and on exposed mountainsides, high winds create a chill factor which makes the cold even more penetrating. In addition, low rainfall and thin, frozen soils, mean that water is scarce. However, many plants manage to survive despite the inhospitable conditions. In the Himalayas, flowering plants have been found at over 6,000 m (20,000 ft), sheltering in hollows in the frost-shattered rock. These plants, known as alpine plants, are generally small and compact, so they can survive on the high mountain peaks, or in the frozen polar regions. Alpine plants often grow in dense cushions or flattened mats, giving them protection against the cold, drying wind. Upright, spreading branches would quickly be battered by the wind, and large leaves would lose valuable heat and water.

A precarious perch for an intrepid alpine plant collector

Mountain avens

Mountain kidney vetch

QUICK WORK
When spring comes, the mountain slopes burst into colour as alpine plants begin to flower. In high mountain areas where the summers are short, these plants have to flower and produce seeds quickly before winter comes around again.

BUILT IN SUN-SCREENS
This mountain kidney vetch, grows high in the Alps, and has leaves covered in hairs. Like those of the silversword, they protect the leaves from sun damage, reduce water loss, and act as insulation.

HAIRY LEAVES
Mountain avens are plants that grow on high ground, from the Alps to the Arctic. Fine hairs on the undersides of their leaves prevent them losing too much water and act as insulation.

RADIATION HAZARD
The sunlight that falls on high mountain tops in the tropics is more intense than anywhere else on Earth. The silversword grows in Hawaii at altitudes of up to 4,000 m (15,000 ft). Its leaves are covered with fine white hairs which protect the plant from much of the sun's dangerous ultraviolet radiation.

PLANT CUSHIONS
This dwarf hebe from New Zealand is an evergreen plant with small tough leaves that can withstand sharp frost. It grows in dense cushions which trap heat, prevent wind damage, and reduce water loss. These cushions are covered in white flowers every spring.

Dwarf hebe

Garland flower

Alpine mo[l]

FLAT AGAINST THE GROUND
Many alpine plants spread over the ground in the form of flat mats, keeping out of the path of icy winds. This "prostrate", or mat-forming plant *Mazus reptans* is from the Himalayas.

Mazus reptans

A MINIATURE SHRUB
This alpine daphne, or garland flower, is a shrub in miniature. Larger daphnes grow at lower levels.

SMALL LEAVES
Moltkias are members of the forget-me-not family. Unlike many of their lowland relatives, alpine moltkias have small leaves which are better able to withstand high winds.

MOUNDS OF COLOUR
Like many alpine plants, this beautiful phlox from North America has brilliantly coloured flowers. They stand out against the rocky slopes and attract pollinating insects.

Alpine phlox

DUAL PROTECTION
Mountain rock roses are protected from the weather in two ways. The bushy plants are able to stand up to strong wind better than those with taller, more rigid stems. Their leaves and stems are covered with fine hairs which act as insulation at night.

Rock rose

TWO WAYS TO SPREAD
This species of storksbill lives in the high Pyrenees. It spreads both with seeds and with its creeping root system (p. 32).

MOUNTAIN DWARF
Many mountain plants which survive at great heights, like this St. John's wort, are much smaller than their lowland relatives.

St. John's wort

Storksbill

51

Living without water

No PLANT CAN LIVE entirely without water, but in very dry regions, where water is scarce, some plants, called cacti and succulents, are able to survive for a number of years between rainstorms. In the world's driest places, rain often comes in irregular but heavy bursts, so the plants that live there have evolved ways of collecting as much water as possible during downpours. The water is then stored in preparation for the next drought. Many cacti and succulents have very long roots, most of which grow near the surface, so that when it rains, they can collect water from a wide area. Once the water is inside the plant, it is kept there by a number of special adaptations. Plants normally lose water from stomata, tiny pores in the leaf surface. The plant can control these pores and keeps them closed if it begins to lose too much water. Many cacti and succulents open the pores only at night, when the air is cool and less water can evaporate. Some of these plants have got around the problem of water loss by losing their leaves altogether.

Mammillaria elongata

Ferocactus

Echinocereus

Fake flowers stuck on by a clever florist to enhance the plant's appearance

Cross-section of square stem

THE CACTUS FAMILY
Almost all true cacti come from the Americas. Because they live in very dry places, they have had to evolve strange shapes to be able to survive. Most cacti have very thick stems and thick groups of spines instead of normal leaves. These spines may protect the plant from heat and cold, as well as from attack by animals. Many cacti have ridges down their stems to allow them to expand and store water when it rains.

Row of spines

SIMILAR SHAPES FOR SIMILAR LIFESTYLES
Not all the spiny plants that live in dry places are cacti. The cactus-like plant on the far left is actually a spurge, a plant quite unrelated to the two cacti to its right. Like the cacti, it has lost its leaves and developed a tough, water-holding stem. This is a typical example of "convergent evolution", in which plants or animals in similar environments evolve in similar ways.

Clusters of spines

Spurge

Prickly pear cactus

Cleistocactus

Cross-section of round stem

THE GIANT SAGUARO
The saguaro is one of the world's tallest cacti. A 250-year-old plant can be 20 m (60 ft) high and can weigh 6 tonnes.

Succulents

Plants with fleshy leaves or stems for storing water are known as succulents and include the group of plants called cacti. There are three main types of succulent. Stem succulents, such as cacti, store water in their stems, and tend to live in the driest climates. Leaf succulents, some of which are shown on this page, store water in their leaves and grow in damper conditions. Finally, root succulents have thickened roots which serve as water reservoirs.

Blue echeveria

The leaves of this species of *Cotyledon* are fleshy, with a waxy surface, to reduce water loss

The whitish "bloom" on the surface of the leaves of *Senecio atandroi* protects the plant from the harsh rays of the sun

LEAF SUCCULENTS
Leaf succulent plants live in semi-desert and also in salt marshes, where the salty conditions mean that fresh water has to be carefully conserved. In prolonged dry weather their leaves wrinkle up. When it rains, they swell as the plant takes in water.

The plump leaves of Haworthia cymbiformis *are swollen with stored water*

Blue echeveria

Haworthia cymbiformis

The necklace vine gets its name from its leaves, which look as if they have been threaded on a string

Kalanchoe tomentosa

Kalanchoe tomentosa

Senecio atandroi

Cotyledon

Necklace vine

LEAVES THAT WITHSTAND DROUGHT
As much as nine-tenths of the weight of a succulent leaf may be stored water. To conserve this vital store, the leaves have a waxy surface which cuts down transpiration, the process by which leaves lose water. Some succulent leaves have a woolly surface which helps to keep the leaf cool, reducing water loss. Succulent leaves have evolved in many unrelated plant species throughout the dry regions of the world.

FLEETING FLOWERS
Many desert plants are "ephemerals". This means that they germinate only after rain and then complete their life cycle very rapidly. For a few days after rain, the desert is ablaze with their flowers. This sea of little yellow flowers is made up of thousands of sand sunflowers, which have all come into bloom at once in the Utah desert.

Food from plants

PLANTS HAVE BEEN CULTIVATED as food crops for thousands of years. The earliest humans lived in nomadic groups, roaming the countryside in search of food. Eventually, these peoples settled down and instead of collecting plant foods from the wild they began to cultivate them. When the time came to gather seeds to produce crops for the following year, they tended to take seeds from the healthiest plants. As they did this year after year, they began to produce better crop plants. Later, more deliberate efforts were made to improve crops by selecting and cultivating the strongest plants, and this process is continuing today. As farming settlements were established independently in different parts of the world, so different crops were cultivated in each place. This meant that when early travellers first visited distant continents, they found many new and exciting foods to bring home. The crops we eat today come from many different parts of the world.

MARKET IN PERU
Potatoes originated in the high Andes of South America. Many varieties of potato are still grown there, as this market scene shows.

KEPT IN THE DARK
If allowed to grow in the light, chicory has a bitter taste. To reduce this bitterness, the plant is cut back to the ground and then allowed to regrow with almost no light. The pale, "blanched" leaves of the new chicory shoot are far less bitter. If cultivated chicory were grown entirely in the light, the plant would look very similar to its ancestor.

Primitive form of corn plant and cob

Blanched shoot of cultivated chicory

Modern corn cob

Wild chicory

PRIMITIVE CORN
Maize is a cereal: like wheat and rice it is a member of the grass family. It was first cultivated in Central America, and some primitive forms of maize can still be found growing there. As a result of selective breeding, the size and shape of the modern corn cob have been increased.

Fruits of a wild tomato, from Mexico

Flowers of wild tomato: flowers of cultivated tomato are very similar

Wild cabbage has dark green, leathery leaves

LEAVING THE PAST BEHIND
The wild cabbage grows near the sea. It has leathery leaves, loosely arranged on a branched stem. Years of breeding have got rid of the plant's bitter taste, and made its leaves more juicy. The shape of the plant has also changed so that, in most cultivated cabbages, the leaves are packed tightly together. In the "red" varieties of cabbage, certain natural pigments have been built up as a result of selective breeding.

Beefsteak tomato

Cultivated tomatoes have become much bigger through breeding

BIGGER - AND BETTER?
The tomato's wild ancestor is a red berry the size of a small grape. It is much sweeter than the modern tomato, and more strongly flavoured.

GROWING IN WATER
Rice, which was cultivated in the Far East at least 5,000 years ago, forms the staple cereal diet of over one half of the world's population. It usually grows in fields of standing water, known as paddy fields.

Flower head of wild carrot

Working in the paddy fields

Modern cabbage

Wild carrot root

Cultivated carrot

EDIBLE ROOTS
The wild carrot is found all over Europe and through much of Asia, but its roots are white or only slightly coloured. Only in Afghanistan is there a variety of wild carrot with orange roots. The carrot was probably first cultivated in that region, and then introduced to other parts of the world.

Modern red cabbage

CARROTS AND CABBAGES
This detail from a 16th-century painting by the Dutch artist Lucas Van Valkenborch proves that even 400 years ago there was a wide variety of vegetables available.

The story of wheat

WHEAT HAS BEEN CULTIVATED by humans as a valuable source of food for at least 9,000 years. Grains of wheat have been found preserved in ancient Egyptian tombs, and it is known that it was the chief cereal of the ancient Greeks and Romans. The cultivation of wheat originated in the region known as the Fertile Crescent, which includes part of Israel, Turkey, Iraq, and Iran. Once a rich farming area, today much of it is desert. Wheat is now grown in most parts of the world and the quality has improved greatly. The early, primitive species, such as einkorn and emmer had long thin stalks which were easily broken in bad weather. The small grains meant that a large number of plants only produced a relatively low yield of grain. Today, as a result of extensive breeding programmes, better varieties have been found which have higher yields, resist drought, and withstand disease.

FOOD FOR THE MASSES
People have grown cereals for food for thousands of years, as this picture from the 11th century shows.

CUTTING THE CORN
Wild grasses drop their ripe seeds. The first farmers selected plants that held on to the seeds, so that the grain could be harvested.

Grains of wild einkorn

Grains of emmer

WILD EINKORN
This wild grass is probably one of the ancestors of all cultivated wheats. It has long, thin stalks and small heads and grains.

EINKORN
This early wheat species is still grown in parts of Turkey for animal feed. Its grains are small and difficult to thresh.

WILD EMMER
This wild grass is the ancestor of emmer, another primitive wheat. The heads and grains are larger than those of einkorn.

EMMER
Emmer was the chief cereal in ancient Greek and Roman times. It is one of the ancestors of modern cultivated wheats.

The long, spiky bristles attached to scales around each grain are called awns

WHEATFIELD PRAIRIE
Today's wheat is much shorter than that of a century ago. Breeders have reduced the amount of stalk, so that the plant does not bend over, making it difficult to harvest the grain. This is an important step forward for the major grain-producing countries of the world, where vast areas of wheat are grown.

Spelt grains

SPELT
The great leap forward for wheats came when emmer crossed, or hybridized, with wild goat grass that was growing as a weed in wheat fields. The result was spelt wheat, which is still cultivated in parts of northwest Europe.

Durum wheat

Brown bread baked with unbleached wholemeal flour

Pasta shells

DURUM WHEAT
Another large-grain wheat closely related to emmer is durum, or macaroni, wheat. It is grown widely today to provide the flour for pasta and biscuits. Because its gluten content is low, it does not make good bread. Modern durum wheat has bigger grains as a result of intensive breeding.

Uncooked wholemeal flour

Bread wheat

BREAD WHEAT
Bread wheat is also a hybrid between emmer and wild goat grass and is the most widely grown modern wheat. Its large grains have a high gluten content which makes bread dough elastic and enables light, airy bread to be made.

White bread, made from very finely ground flour that has been bleached

Potions and poisons

IN ANCIENT TIMES, plants were the main source of medicines. By trial and error, it was discovered that particular species could cure certain diseases. These plants were often grown in special gardens, and their details noted in herbals. Today, many plants are still used by the pharmaceutical industry. The chemicals they produce may be poisonous in large quantities, but small amounts can prove very useful in the treatment of some illnesses. The search for new medicines continues today, and every year pharmacologists examine thousands of plants from all over the world.

MANDRAKE
The mandrake root, once used in medicines, sometimes looks almost human. It was usually pulled up by a dog, because, according to an old superstition, the root would shriek as it came out of the ground. Any human who heard the noise would die.

Red ginseng root from Korea

OUT OF THE EAST
In China, ginseng has been prized for about 5,000 years. The powdered root has a stimulant effect, and can aid recovery from illness. Ginseng is grown commercially and is now sold all over the world.

Aloe vera

Jojoba

Cosmetic preparation made from aloe vera

COSMETIC EFFECT
Plants are often used in cosmetics for their pleasant smell, or soothing oils. Two plants that are popular in today's cosmetics are jojoba and aloe vera. Both live in dry places and contain oils that help to keep skin soft.

Opium poppies growing in Turkey

THE OPIUM POPPY
For thousands of years opium poppies have been grown as a source of drugs. Raw opium is the poppy's dried sap. It oozes out of the unripe seed head after it has been scarred with a knife. Opium is used in the manufacture of morphine, codeine, and heroin - drugs which can be deadly if misused.

Beans contain oil and poisonous ricin

Detail of a page from a 12th-century herbal

A gweri siquidem dr cocosindos.
Quidam ú camellam eam uocát.

Castor-oil plant

A DEADLY DOSE
The oil from the beans of the castor-oil plant has been used to purify the system since the days of the ancient Egyptians. The beans also contain ricin, one of the most potent poisons known. Ricin is so powerful that, if eaten, just one bean is enough to kill an adult.

Leaves of the "dumb cane"

THE DUMB CANE
The name of this plant comes from its poisonous sap. If this is swallowed, it makes the mouth swell so much that talking becomes difficult.

DRINK, OR DRUG?
The mescal cactus *Lophophora williamsii* contains a hallucinogenic substance called mescaline, which is used in the religious rituals of certain Mexican Indian tribes. Confusingly, the Mexican drink mescal is not derived from the mescal cactus *Lophophora*, but from another Mexican plant, *Agave tequilana*.

Mescal cactus

The drink mescal is made from the plant *Agave tequilana*

DEADLY BERRIES
The drug atropine, which is used in eye surgery and to treat stomach complaints, is derived from a very poisonous plant called belladonna, or deadly nightshade.

FROM COCA TO COCAINE
Many centuries ago, South American Indians discovered that chewing the leaves of the coca plant dulled pain and prevented tiredness. Coca leaves contain the drug cocaine. Although a valuable anaesthetic, cocaine can be dangerously addictive.

Coca leaves for sale

Coca leaves

Foxglove

This group in India at the end of the 19th century are relaxing with a gin and tonic

Belladonna, or deadly nightshade

HELP FOR THE HEART
The leaves of the foxglove contain a substance that is used to treat heart conditions. In large doses, it produces palpitations and dizziness, but in smaller doses, it helps the heart to beat more slowly and strongly.

A CURE FOR MALARIA
Quinine, which is used in the treatment of malaria, is obtained from the bark of South American cinchona trees. Quinine is also used as a bitter flavour in tonic water, a drink which is commonly mixed with gin.

Cinchona leaves

The plant collectors

A 19th-century plant collector with his collecting case, or vasculum

Many of the plants that have become common in gardens all over the world are, in fact, very far from home. Most fuchsias, for example, come originally from South America, wisteria from China and Japan, many azaleas from the Himalayas, and tulips from western and central Asia. These are just some of the thousands of plants that have been carried across the world by plant collectors. Plant collecting had its heyday in the 19th and early 20th centuries, as intrepid botanists travelled farther and farther afield in search of unknown plants. Some plant collectors experienced great hardships on their voyages to distant places - being shot at, caught in earthquakes, and attacked by wild animals. But despite all such adversities, the lure of making new discoveries spurred them on to explore some of the world's most remote and dangerous places.

Scutellaria tournefortia is named after its discoverer Joseph Pitton de Tournefort

ROYAL MISSION
Joseph Pitton de Tournefort (1656-1708) was a botanist who was sent to the eastern Mediterranean by the French king Louis XIV. He returned with the specimens and seeds of over a thousand plants, many of which became garden favourites.

A 19th-century vasculum containing *Sarcococca hookeriana*, a species of sweet box, one of many plants named after the Hookers

GOING EAST
The photograph above shows botanists on a plant-collecting expedition to China in the 1920s. This region of the world has been of great interest to botanists for many years, and expeditions made there today still discover new plant species. The photograph on the right shows a botanist on a modern plant-collecting expedition.

FATHER AND SON
William Hooker (1785-1865) and his son Joseph (1817-1911) were both passionately interested in plants. William Hooker became the first director of The Royal Botanic Gardens at Kew in England. Joseph is especially remembered for collecting many species of rhododendron in the Himalayas.

Leaves of
plane tree

Tradescant
father
and son

GOING WEST
John Tradescant and his son, also named John,
were English plantsmen. Tradescant the elder
collected in Russia, and Tradescant the younger
collected in America. The younger Tradescant
imported trees into Europe. These included the
tulip tree and the western plane.

FIT FOR ROYALTY
Plant collecting is an ancient pursuit. This
Egyptian mural shows the earliest recorded
expedition, which took place in 1495 B.C.
Collectors brought back frankincense trees for
Queen Hatshepsut from the Horn of Africa.

Tradescantia - a
border plant named
after John Tradescant
the elder

Beautifully preserved
botanical reference books

THE EMPRESS COLLECTOR
Empress Josephine, the wife of
Napoleon, created a unique garden at
her house at Malmaison, with roses
brought from all around the world. At
the time France was at war with
Britain, but ships carrying the imperial
roses were allowed safe passage.

Looking at plants

Herbarium
specimen
sheet

PLANT COLLECTIONS are of two kinds - living plants and preserved specimens. The preserved specimens are mostly pressed, and are kept in a herbarium, where they can be examined by botanists. Collections of living plants are equally important, and sometimes ensure that rare plant species do not die out. Making your own collection of flowers and pressing them is a good way to learn about plants. However, you should not pick flowers that are growing wild in the countryside, as this prevents them from producing seeds. All wild flower species are protected by law, and you must not uproot them without receiving permission from the person who owns the land. If you want to try to grow your own plants, you can collect small amounts of seed, or you can buy wild flower seeds, produced by plants that have been raised in nurseries. Growing your own plants gives you a chance to study them without harming plants in the wild.

Preserving
bottle

Box
containing
dried specimen

HERB. HORT. REG. B

Na echinacea

Forest, Lincs

HERB. HORT. BOT. REG. KEW.

4781

Dendrobium (lindleyi) aggregatum Rol

Thailand

Menzies & July
89

Plant press

BOTANIST'S COLLECTING EQUIPMENT
When collecting plants for the herbarium, a specimen is pressed and then mounted on a herbarium sheet with a label saying where and when it was found. The herbarium sheet can then be consulted by botanists wishing to study the plant in detail

Secateurs

Trowel

Sketch pad

Magnifying glass

LEARNING MORE ABOUT PLANTS

One of the best ways of finding out more about wild flowers is to draw or photograph them. If you draw them, you will notice many details about their structure, which will help you to identify the plant family. A magnifying glass is very useful for examining leaves and petals more closely. Collecting seeds and growing plants from them requires patience and care. Stored seeds should always be kept dry. Many seeds will germinate better if they are left in a refrigerator for a few weeks before planting. This cold period simulates the low winter temperatures they may experience in the wild. Large seeds, like those from sweet peas, germinate more quickly if they are first scratched, or "scarified", with sandpaper.

Scissors

Camera

Envelopes for collecting seed

PRESERVING SPECIMENS

Plants and their flowers can be pressed with a simple screw press, or even a pile of books. In both cases, the specimens are laid between two sheets of absorbent paper which should be changed for dry sheets every day or so. It can take several weeks for specimens to dry out.

Top for plant press

Plant press

Screws for tightening plant press

Index

Acknowledgments

Dorling Kindersley would like to thank:
Brinsley Burbidge, Valerie Whalley, John Lonsdale, Milan Swaderlig, Andrew McRobb, Marilyn Ward and Pat Griggs of the Royal Botanic Gardens, Kew.
Arthur Chater at the Natural History Museum.
Dave King for special photography on pages 8-9.
Fred Ford and Mike Pilley at Radius for artwork.

Picture credits

t=top b=bottom m=middle l=left r=right

A-Z Botanical: 55m
Heather Angel/Biofotos: 43tm; 49ml
V. Angel/Daily Telegraph Colour Library: 39bm
Australian High Commission: 24tr; 57tr
A.N.T./NHPA: 25mr
J. and M. Bain/NHPA: 11bl
G.I. Bernard/Oxford Scientific Films: 7tl; 46br
G.I. Bernard/NHPA: 15tr; 18mr; 36m; 40mr
Bridgeman Art Library: 55mb; 58br
Brinsley Burbidge/Royal Botanic Gardens, Kew: 50bm; 58m
M.Z. Capell/ZEFA: 10tr
James H. Carmichael/NHPA: 53br

Gene Cox/Science Photo Library: 7m
Stephen Dalton/NHPA: 19tr; 22ml; 30tl; 36tr; 40ml
P. Dayanandan/Science Photo Library: 9tl
Jack Dermid/Oxford Scientific Films: 32br
Dr. Dransfield/Royal Botanic Gardens, Kew: 45
Mary Evans Picture Library: 44tl; 46bl; 48ml; 56tl, tr; 60tr; 61br; 62tm
Robert Francis/South American Pictures: 54tl
Linda Gamlin: 27mr; 29bm
Brian Hawkes/NHPA: 23tl
Hulton Picture Library: 42tl
E.A. Janes/NHPA: 28bl
Patrick Lynch/Science Photo Library: 6tm; 8br
Mansell Collection: 8bl; 59bm
Marion Morrison/South American

Pictures: 59m
Peter Newark'sWestern Americana: 52br
Brian M. Rogers/Biofotos: 46bm
Royal Botanic Gardens, Kew: 16tl; 43tl; 60m; 61m
John Shaw/NHPA: 9tr
Survival Anglia: 7tl
John Walsh/Science Photo Library: 15tl
J. Watkins/Frank Lane Picture Agency: 50bl
Roger Wilmshurst/Frank Lane: 26tr

Illustrations by: Sandra Pond and Will Giles: 12-13, 17, 38

Picture research by Angela Jones